The Pursuit of Knowledge

The Pursuit of Knowledge

Speeches and Papers of Richard C. Atkinson

Patricia A. Pelfrey, editor

With a foreword by David S. Saxon

UNIVERSITY OF CALIFORNIA PRESS

Berkeley   Los Angeles   London

University of California Press, one of the most distinguished
university presses in the United States, enriches lives around the
world by advancing scholarship in the humanities, social sciences,
and natural sciences. Its activities are supported by the UC Press
Foundation and by philanthropic contributions from individuals
and institutions. For more information, visit www.ucpress.edu.

University of California Press
Berkeley and Los Angeles, California

University of California Press, Ltd.
London, England

Library of Congress Cataloging-in-Publication Data

Atkinson, Richard C.
    The pursuit of knowledge : speeches and papers of Richard C.
Atkinson / edited by Patricia Pelfrey ; with a foreword by David
S. Saxon.
        p.   cm.
    Includes bibliographical references and index.
    ISBN: 978-0-520-25199-1 (pbk. : alk. paper)
    1. University of California, Berkeley.   2. Universities and
colleges—Administration.   3. Education, Higher—United States—
Aims and objectives.   4. Atkinson, Richard C.   5. College
presidents—California—Biography.   I. Pelfrey, Patricia A.
II. Title.
LD736.5.A85   2007
378'.050974—dc22   2006025557

Manufactured in the United States of America

16   15   14   13   12   11   10   09   08   07
10   9   8   7   6   5   4   3   2   1

This book is printed on New Leaf EcoBook 50, a 100% recycled
fiber of which 50% is de-inked post-consumer waste, processed
chlorine-free. EcoBook 50 is acid-free and meets the minimum
requirements of ANSI/ASTM D5634–01 (Permanence of Paper).

CONTENTS

FOREWORD

There are two ways of judging the accomplishments of university presidents: by the battles they have won and the battles they have fought. The battles won are reflected in such bottom-line measures as the size of the institutional budget and the distinction of the faculty. From this vantage point, Richard Atkinson's tenure as president of the University of California was rich in victories. But understanding the ideas and ideals of a particular presidency requires a far broader perspective—a sense of the battles a president has faced as well as the battles that have been won. These live on in a president's public speeches and papers. As this volume makes clear, President Atkinson fought on behalf of many causes crucial to the University during his eight-year administration. Let me mention two of truly major significance.

The first is the enduring conundrum of race and affirmative action. No other issue in American life presents as challenging a combination of democratic idealism, conflicting views, and persistent pressures from across the political spectrum. Every

U.C. president since Clark Kerr (1958–67) has had to struggle with the educational and demographic imperative of including within the University more members of traditionally excluded groups. Richard Atkinson was the first who had to address it without the advantage of admissions programs and policies that explicitly recognize race and its profound implications for access to education. He inherited the leadership of the University just weeks after it had become the nation's first institution of higher education to ban the use of race and ethnicity as factors in admissions and hiring.

The question of race is still with us; it remains the intractable problem of our time. But President Atkinson made a major contribution to California and U.C. by accomplishing what had to be done—moving the University into a radically different world of race-neutral policies and practices—without sacrificing either the University's commitment to all the students of this state or its dedication to high academic standards. It was a difficult process that would have been even more difficult without his leadership.

Affirmative action was an inescapable challenge for the Atkinson presidency. The use and misuse of standardized admissions tests—the second major issue President Atkinson confronted—was not. By 2001, American higher education's reliance on the SAT I aptitude test had gone effectively unchallenged for seventy-five years, even though no one has ever proved that aptitude tests actually measure innate abilities, or that so complex a phenomenon as intelligence can be captured in a single number. A national debate about the limits and possibilities of standardized testing, and especially the claims of the SAT I, was urgently needed and long overdue. President Atkinson's announcement in February 2001 that he was recommending elimination of the SAT I as a requirement for admission to U.C. galvanized that indispensable debate. As president of a great public university that was also the country's largest user of the SAT I, President Atkinson had the institutional influence to focus national attention on the issue. As a distinguished cognitive scientist, he had the professional credentials to make a compelling case for reform. And—not least—he had the courage to take on a large and controversial issue that, despite its deep importance, had suffered from decades of neglect. His insistence that standardized tests must be carefully designed and thoughtfully employed has had a nationwide impact.

This record of the Atkinson presidency serves as an introduction to eight eventful years in the life of the University and American higher education. It is also an introduction to the president himself—his remarkable energy, his perennially youthful enthusiasm, and his firm vision of what a research university ought to be. I am pleased to have played a role in persuading him to accept the chancellorship of U.C. San Diego in 1980. The rest is history—and a matter of great good fortune for the University of California.

David S. Saxon
President Emeritus
University of California

EDITOR'S NOTE

The contents of this volume have been selected from a larger digital collection of speeches, papers, statements, and other writings associated with the 1995–2003 administration of University of California president Richard C. Atkinson. A few documents have been edited to clarify or bring references up to date. "College Admissions and the SAT: A Personal Perspective," a paper that President Emeritus Atkinson presented to the American Educational Research Association in April 2004, is included here because of the light it sheds on his proposal regarding the SAT and the College Board's decision to revise the test.

The digital collection of speeches and other papers from the Atkinson presidency can be found in the California Digital Library's eScholarship Repository at http://repositories.cdlib.org/escholarship/. Special thanks are due to the University of California Press and the California Digital Library for their generous help and support with this book and with the digital collection. I also wish to thank Robert Menzimer for his professional skill and assistance as a copy editor for the entire project. And I want to express my appreciation to President Emeritus Atkinson for his cooperation throughout this effort.

President Emeritus David S. Saxon died in December 2005, a few months after completing the foreword to this book. His legacy of thoughtful and courageous leadership is a reminder of why university presidents matter to the institutions they serve. I am pleased and deeply grateful that his words introduce this volume.

Patricia A. Pelfrey
Center for Studies in Higher Education
Berkeley, California

A Brief History of
the Atkinson Presidency

1995–2003

The issues that dominated the administration of Richard C. Atkinson grew out of the forces shaping California: the state's emergence as the world's leading knowledge-based economy and the rapidly expanding size and diversity of its population, which brought the largest student generation since the 1960s to the University's door. Atkinson's administrative and intellectual leadership of the University reflected a deliberate effort to define U.C.'s role in this changing California.

Atkinson led the University into the post-affirmative-action era and American education into a new chapter in the history of standardized testing as the seventeenth president of the nation's leading multicampus system. His eight-year tenure was marked by innovative approaches to admissions and outreach, research initiatives to accelerate the University's contributions to the state's economy, and a challenge to the country's most widely used admissions examination—the SAT I—that paved the way to major change in how millions of young Americans are tested for college admission.

The Atkinson years will be remembered as a time of great growth and prosperity, a period during which U.C.'s state-funded budget rose to historic highs and federal research funding and private giving regularly set new records. The University named the founding chancellor for U.C. Merced, its first new campus in forty years. It established several new professional schools and initiated growth in its graduate programs with a plan for the addition of eleven thousand graduate students by 2010. Nine University chancellors were appointed during Atkinson's presidency.

The University of California also expanded its national presence with a new center in Washington, D.C., and its international reach with centers in London and Mexico City. The establishment of the California Digital Library, a pioneering effort to make the University's vast collections more accessible to scholars and the public and to encourage new forms of scholarly communication, reflected the University's leadership in the evolving world of digital telecommunications.

Atkinson's principal priority was maintaining the distinction of U.C.'s seven-thousand-member faculty. The academic excellence of the University and its faculty was recognized in several national studies of academic program quality, one of which noted "the extraordinary research performance of the entire University of California system" among American universities, public and private.[1] The membership of six out of nine U.C. general campuses in the prestigious Association of American Universities exceeds that of any other multicampus system. Eleven U.C.

faculty members were awarded Nobel Prizes during Atkinson's tenure, more than under any other U.C. president.

As chancellor of U.C. San Diego from 1980 to 1995, during which time the young campus rose to rank tenth among American research universities, Atkinson combined driving energy and a gift for persuasion with an unswerving pursuit of his goals. As president of the U.C. System, he attacked the University's problems and opportunities with the same persistent vigor.

Atkinson faced his share of crises and controversies, among them an early and public disagreement with some members of the Board of Regents over the implementation date of SP-1, the ban on using race and ethnicity as factors in U.C. admission. UCSF Stanford Healthcare, the merger of the clinical enterprises of U.C. San Francisco and Stanford University, was a historic but ultimately unsuccessful attempt to address the competitive pressures of the health-care marketplace. California's sudden transition from prosperity to recession toward the end of Atkinson's tenure confronted the University with painful choices. And U.C.'s administration of the U.S. Department of Energy (DOE) laboratory at Los Alamos, New Mexico, came under fire in 2000, resulting in a decision by DOE to put the laboratory's management contract up for competitive bidding in 2005. In the end, however, U.C.'s bid for renewal of its contract with DOE was successful.

SP-1 AND U.C. OUTREACH

Atkinson's earliest and greatest challenge was in the contentious arena of U.C. admissions. He was named president in August 1995. A month earlier, the Board of Regents had approved SP-1, which put U.C. in the national spotlight. The ban on racial preferences was extended to all public entities in California sixteen months later with the passage of Proposition 209.

For U.C.'s president and chancellors, SP-1 and Proposition 209 were an exacting test of leadership in reversing three decades of race-attentive policies while also ensuring that U.C., as a public university in the nation's most diverse state, continued to be seen as a welcoming place for minority students. Under Atkinson's guidance, the University dramatically expanded its partnerships with the K-12 schools to raise academic achievement throughout California, especially in those districts with high proportions of academically disadvantaged students. At Governor Gray Davis's request, and as part of Davis's school reform initiative, the University established the Principal Leadership Institutes, the California Professional Development Institutes, and a series of other initiatives to improve the preparation of California's teachers and K-12 administrators.

With Atkinson's support, the Regents voted to rescind SP-1 in May 2001. The board's resolution affirmed the University's intent to continue complying with Proposition 209's ban on racial preferences while reaffirming U.C.'s commitment to enrolling a student body that reflects both exceptional achievement and "the broad diversity of backgrounds characteristic of California."

RESEARCH FOR A DYNAMIC ECONOMY

Atkinson came to the U.C. presidency convinced that twenty-first-century science requires new forms of organization and funding. In particular, his goal was to tap the enormous potential within the University for research that serves the needs of

California's economy. One of his first acts as president was to establish the Industry-University Cooperative Research Program (IUCRP) to promote research partnerships with industry in disciplines critical to the state's economic competitiveness. The IUCRP is now a 280-million-dollar enterprise that supports nearly six hundred projects, jointly supported by state, U.C., and industry funds, in areas ranging from biotechnology to digital media.

To address a looming crisis in the state's supply of engineers and computer scientists, in 1997 Atkinson committed the University to increasing enrollments in those fields 50 percent by 2005–06. U.C. exceeded this goal in 2002, four years ahead of schedule, and engineering and computer science enrollments exceeded twenty-seven thousand in 2003–04, up from sixteen thousand in 1997–98. The initiative represents the first real growth in the state's engineering programs since the 1968 Terman Report, whose conclusion that California had an oversupply of programs and facilities in the field brought the expansion of engineering education to a virtual halt.[2]

Governor Davis was an enthusiastic supporter of the University's efforts. In 2000, he asked U.C. to establish four California Institutes for Science and Innovation (CISIs) on its campuses. The institutes bring together industry and university researchers to concentrate on scientific challenges that are ripe for application in the fields of nanotechnology, telecommunications and information technology, biotechnology, and quantitative medicine. The CISIs constitute one of the most far reaching efforts in the nation to create new basic research and education programs and then to link them with a state's entrepreneurial industries through intensive partnerships. To honor President Atkinson's role in the establishment of the institutes and his service to the University, the building that houses the California Institute for Telecommunications and Information Technology (Calit2) on the U.C. San Diego campus has been designated Atkinson Hall.

TIDAL WAVE II AND U.C. ADMISSIONS POLICY

Another challenge of the Atkinson era was preparing the University for a new generation of students—Tidal Wave II, the children of the Baby Boomers. Accommodating its share of Tidal Wave II meant finding a place on U.C. campuses for sixty-three thousand additional students—an enrollment increase of 40 percent—and recruiting thousands of new faculty members between 1998 and 2010. Atkinson initiated a comprehensive planning effort to help the University grow quickly without endangering its quality.

The Atkinson presidency was notable for its intense focus on the issue of educational opportunity, a matter of increasing public and legislative scrutiny because of SP-1 and growing competition for admission to U.C. Atkinson played an active part in reshaping U.C.'s admissions policies and practices to make them, in his words, "demonstrably inclusive and fair." On his recommendation, the University's Academic Senate and the Regents approved several new paths to admission. The purpose of these new approaches was to supplement traditional grades and test scores with broader measures of student achievement, among them what students have made of their opportunities to learn. In addition, undergraduate applicants now receive the kind of comprehensive review of their qualifications usually associated with selective private universities.

ACHIEVEMENT VERSUS APTITUDE

Atkinson has earned a place in the annals of standardized testing for his challenge to higher education's decades-long use of aptitude tests to predict students' readiness for college. He made national headlines in February 2001 when he told the American Council on Education that he had asked the Academic Senate of the University of California to drop the SAT I examination requirement in favor of tests that assess what students actually learn in school rather than "ill-defined notions of aptitude." Atkinson's case for achievement tests was that they are more reliable predictors of future success, fairer to students, and better guides for schools in determining the curriculum.

In June 2002, the College Board, the sponsor of the SAT, announced that beginning in 2005 it would add a written essay and a more rigorous mathematics section to the seventy-six-year-old test. Atkinson welcomed the decision and praised the College Board for having "laid the foundation for a new test that will better serve our students and schools."

THE ATKINSON YEARS

The University's seventeenth president will be remembered for his absolute commitment to faculty quality, his skill in balancing U.C.'s competing pressures and responsibilities, and his resourcefulness in using the opportunities prosperity offered to urge the University in new directions. "The role of knowledge in transforming virtually every aspect of our world has moved research universities to center stage of American life," he once said. This conviction animated the leadership he brought to the University of California and to American higher education.

NOTES

1. Hugh Davis Graham and Nancy Diamond, *The Rise of American Research Universities: Elites and Challengers in the Postwar Era* (Baltimore, MD: Johns Hopkins University Press, 1997), 202.

2. Frederick Terman, "A Study of Engineering Education in California" (Sacramento: Coordinating Council for Higher Education, March 1968). The council, a state agency, is now called the California Postsecondary Education Commission.

Seventeenth President

Remarks on Receiving
the University of Chicago
Alumni Medal

June 2003

It is always a wonderful experience to return to the University of Chicago. The campus was beautiful when I first set eyes upon it in 1944, and even with all the changes, it is still one of the most beautiful and inspiring campuses in the world.

My decision to enroll at the University of Chicago was by pure happenstance. Both of my parents were immigrants to the United States. Neither had much formal education, and in our household, a college education was not high on our list of priorities. But in February of 1944, when I was a sophomore in high school, one of those unplanned events occurred that transforms a person's life. A friend and I had arranged to spend a Saturday playing basketball. When I arrived at his home, his mother greeted me at the front door and explained that he had to cancel out on our plans since arrangements had been made for him to take the college entrance examination at the University of Chicago. I was very disappointed, but then my friend called out from a second-story window—much to his mother's displeasure—that I should go with him to the university and that we would be back in time to salvage the rest of the day. I had nothing better to do and agreed.

We arrived at Cobb Hall. The person in charge had my friend sign in for the examination and then turned to me and asked for my name. "Oh, no," I said, "I'm not on your list and I'm not here to take the exam." He said, "Well, since you're here, you might as well take the exam." So I did. A few weeks later, my friend received a letter of rejection, and I was admitted. Not being sure of what to do, I decided to enroll in the summer session with the idea that I would return to my junior year in high school if all did not go well.

The summer of 1944 was a remarkable time. The Allies landed in Normandy and began the invasion of Europe. The Democrats held their national convention in Chicago, and my roommate at the university was a nephew of Paul McNutt, the Democratic governor of Indiana, who arranged for us to have passes to all of the convention activities. President Roosevelt was seeking nomination for his fourth term as president, and the theme song for the convention was "Don't change horses in midstream." But of course they did make one major change. Wallace was dropped as the vice president in favor of Truman.

That summer my mind was aroused as never before. The courses and faculty were extraordinary, but equally important were the debates long into the night with other students on issues of religion, politics, and race relations (the term used at the time). Once caught up in the intellectual life of the University of Chicago, I never looked back.

My years at the university were a transforming experience and, in a very real sense, defined the rest of my life. I took OII—Observation, Interpretation, and Integration—in a special section taught jointly by President Hutchins and Mortimer Adler. Hutchins was at the peak of his fame, and Adler had played a key role in developing the Great Books program (he was affectionately referred to as "The Great Bookie" by students). We had about a dozen students in the class and the discussions were intense. Even to this day, I consider myself something of an expert on Plato's *Republic*. Allan Bloom, who was a fellow student in that course, later went on to write the well-known book *The Closing of the American Mind*. I took BI/SCI, the biological sciences, from A. J. Carlson, one of the world's great scientists, who was an equally brilliant teacher. His textbook with Johnson, *The Machinery of the Body*, is a classic. My introductory chemistry course was taught by Harold Urey, a Nobel laureate, who later became a lifelong friend. For approximately a year, I roomed in the home of Professor David Riesman, who was famous at the time, but later became even more famous when he wrote *The Lonely Crowd*. He often invited me to parties at his home that included some of the great social scientists of the era. And for some time, I worked as a research assistant for Professor Nicolas Rashevsky, who was involved in formulating mathematical theories of biological and social processes. I did endless computations for him on equations that were basic to his theories. This predated digital computers, and the work was done on a hand-cranked calculator. We ran into real problems that we never quite solved, because the equations proved to be too disorderly. For the mathematicians among you, they were second-order-difference equations, and years later, they were to become part of what is now called "chaos theory." If only I had known then what I know today.

Those were wonderful days that shaped my views about the nature of a great university and the concept of a liberal education. The University of Chicago may not have produced its share of Wall Street financiers or corporate lawyers, but it has produced more than its share of academics. Everywhere I have been—schools, colleges, universities, research institutions, foundations—I have met people educated at the University of Chicago who have made a difference in our society because of their high academic standards and their commitment to excellence.

I spent part of my career in La Jolla, California, at the University of California, San Diego, helping build what has become a world-class institution. And in the building process, the image of the University of Chicago was always very much in my mind. In the early 1960s, when U.C. San Diego expanded from an oceanographic institution to a full-fledged university, those in charge of the university had the wisdom and good fortune to recruit a large number of the founding faculty from the University of Chicago. Those faculty members became the core of the institution, and for many years they had a University of Chicago New Year's party in La Jolla to celebrate their Chicago heritage. Indeed, U.C. San Diego was often referred to as the University of Chicago at San Diego. Harold Urey was in that founding group of faculty, along with Joe Mayer, who was also a world-famous chemist. U.C. San Diego was successful in recruiting Joe because he had a wife, Maria, who was a physicist. But because nepotism rules were still in effect in those days at the University of Chicago, she could not hold a regular academic appointment. Both were recruited to U.C.

San Diego with full academic appointments. And a few years later, Maria Mayer won the Nobel Prize in physics, the second woman in history to win a Nobel Prize. San Diego was not as sophisticated a city in those days as it is today, and the newspaper headlines read, "La Jolla Housewife Wins Nobel Prize."

Finally, let me briefly comment on the SAT college entrance exam. As you probably know, the test will undergo a fundamental change effective for students entering college in the fall of 2006—three years from now. In the 1940s, there was an interesting debate among academics about the nature of college entrance examinations. The principal focal points of this debate were at Harvard University and the University of Chicago. To oversimplify matters, President James Bryant Conant of Harvard University and his colleagues advocated for a test designed to measure aptitude, whereas the Chicago contingent argued for a test designed to measure achievement. Conant's perspective won the day, and with it came the widespread adoption of the SAT. Conant later in life expressed regrets about his role in promoting the SAT, but it was too late. With the changes that go into effect in the fall of 2006, the SAT will be reinvented in the form that the Chicago group advocated many years ago. It is a long overdue change that I believe will have a fundamental effect on K-12 education and will be a more useful device for judging whether a student is prepared to do college-level work.

Once again, let me say how wonderful it is to be back at the University of Chicago. And how honored I am to be awarded the Alumni Medal.

The Golden Fleece,
Science Education, and
U.S. Science Policy

November 1997

I was pleased to accept Roger Hahn's kind invitation to participate in this colloquium series. It gave me an opportunity to rethink some events I was associated with at the National Science
Foundation [NSF] in the 1970s. I would like to review briefly
U.S. science policy since World War II from the perspective of
the National Science Foundation, and in particular from the
narrower perspective of science education and the social sciences at NSF. This is a personal account, not a scholarly one,
and I would be delighted if my remarks were to stimulate some
aspiring young historians to undertake a more careful study of
the events I am going to discuss.

My story begins with World War II and the remarkable success of U.S. science in the war effort—a critical factor in our vic-
tory. President Roosevelt's science adviser, Vannevar Bush, had

been a long-term member of the faculty at the Massachusetts Institute of Technology; he was one of the key people responsible for building the quality of that institution. Bush had a close personal relationship with Roosevelt. Near the end of the war the president asked him to define a plan for American science in the postwar period. That request led to Bush's landmark report, *Science: The Endless Frontier,* one of the great documents of American history. The Bush report defined science policy for the post–World War II era.

What was the nature of that report? No summary could do justice to Bush's masterful analysis, but essentially he made three principal arguments about the future of the U.S. scientific enterprise. First, he argued that most aspects of research and development [R&D] were the responsibility of the private sector. But he also recognized that market mechanisms would discourage the private sector from investing adequate funds in basic research. This led Bush to his second argument: ensuring support for basic research in the postwar period should be the responsibility of the federal government, because the enormous benefits to society at large justified the investment. He did not believe basic research should be conducted in government laboratories, however, but in the universities of the nation. As the institutions responsible for the nation's basic research, universities had pride of place in Bush's vision of the research enterprise. Third, he argued that decisions about which university research projects the government would fund should be made via a peer-review process.

Bush envisioned a federal agency that would be responsible for funding these research activities. Legislation was introduced in 1945, but because of disagreements between the Truman administration and Congress, as well as within the Congress itself, the National Science Foundation was not created until May 1950. The events of this five-year period are nicely described in an excellent recent biography of Vannevar Bush by G. Pascal Zachary [*Endless Frontier: Vannevar Bush, Engineer of the American Century*].

One of the debates surrounding that legislation involved the scope of the foundation's proposed activities. Harry Truman was now president. His associates urged a broader range of responsibilities for the foundation than Bush's supporters did, one that included science education and the social sciences. Bush, on the other hand, had only minimal interest in including science education and no interest at all in including the social sciences. James Conant, a close colleague of Bush renowned for his reorganization of Harvard's general education curriculum, was a strong proponent of including science education on NSF's agenda. In the end, Conant's view prevailed. Science education became one of NSF's responsibilities. So did the social sciences, but without a clear mandate to fund them.

NSF got off to an extremely slow start, with minimal funding in the various sciences. There was a trickle of science education activities in the early years, but they were almost wholly confined to supporting fellowship programs for graduate students. Bush and many other leading scientists of that period felt NSF was not meeting their initial expectations and viewed the agency as of little consequence.

The world changed in October 1957, when Sputnik was launched. The public response bordered on panic: there was much alarmed discussion of an education gap—an ominous disparity between the quality of American science education and its counterpart in the Soviet Union. Within a month, the administration established the President's Science Advisory Committee [PSAC], which played a very important role in the Eisenhower, Kennedy, and Johnson administrations. Congress responded with the National Defense Education Act, which dramatically increased federal funding for student loan programs and graduate fellowships in science and engineering, among other things. In the post-Sputnik years, support for science climbed rapidly, and funding for NSF took off. Gradually the activities in the social sciences increased, until 1968, [when] legislation was introduced to change the NSF Organic Act to require funding in these disciplines.

In particular, science education blossomed. NSF began offering summer institutes for K-12 teachers, in which leading university scientists met with teachers to discuss scientific developments and how to teach them. Even more important were curriculum development projects. Few people trusted the Office of Education to carry out this responsibility; NSF was the agency everyone turned to. NSF started in physics, with a curriculum developed by Jerrold Zacharias of MIT, and a mathematics curriculum quickly followed. So did a program in chemistry; faculty at U.C. Berkeley played an important role in developing the chemistry curriculum. One can criticize these programs. They were too difficult for the average student—too focused on the best students—but the simple fact is that if you go anywhere in the world today, you will find that these programs are still in use and are regarded as outstanding curricula.

The curriculum projects went so well that NSF decided to be even bolder. It ventured into the biological sciences and began to develop and distribute biology courses to the high schools. Teachers were given special training, and the curricula were widely used. Eventually these curricula expanded to include topics on evolution, which brought out the creationists in force. They criticized NSF's involvement both as undermining religious beliefs and as a federal intrusion into local authority. But the loudest outcry was reserved for a social science curriculum called Man: A Course of Study [MACOS]. MACOS was developed under the intellectual leadership of Jerome Bruner, who was at Harvard at that time.

MACOS focused on cultural diversity, principally from an anthropological viewpoint, and was aimed at students in grades seven, eight, and nine. One of the films produced for the course told the story of an Eskimo village above the Arctic Circle. Among the Eskimo practices depicted in the film was the custom of borrowing someone else's wife to keep you warm on a long journey across the ice if your own wife was not well enough to accompany you. Another was the practice of abandoning grandparents on an ice floe when they became too old to contribute. MACOS succeeded brilliantly in demonstrating cultural differences; it was equally effective in arousing public outrage. There were protest rallies, public meetings at schools that adopted MACOS, and vitriolic editorials—Jim Kilpatrick [a conservative newspaper columnist] wrote extensively on the damage MACOS was inflicting by undermining the moral character of America's young people.

Around this time Senator William Proxmire began presenting Golden Fleece awards for instances of government fraud, waste, or abuse. An early award went to the Air Force for spending two thousand dollars per toilet seat for bombers. But soon Proxmire's interest shifted to NSF, and the agency became a perfect target. One of the early awards was a Golden Fleece for a research grant entitled "The Sexual Behavior of the

Screw-Worm Fly." Proxmire got tremendous attention for that; I'll return to it a little later.

When he delved into the social sciences, he found an NSF-supported grant dealing with an experimental analysis of love from a social/psychological perspective and another grant concerned with a theory of love. At that time, the *National Enquirer* was paying a five-hundred-dollar bounty to freelance reporters who came up with a story of this sort, and many writers would just scan the titles of research projects supported by NSF. The *Chicago Tribune* had a field day with the theory of love grant, and as if this weren't bad enough, they found a project titled "A Theory of Necking Behavior." We tried in vain to find this grant on NSF's list of social science projects. Days later we finally unearthed it among the engineering projects—the necking referred to was of a metal, not a human, variety.

Several of the faculty grantees who were recipients of the Golden Fleece wore it proudly as a badge of merit and made the most of their notoriety on the Johnny Carson show. This was serious business for NSF, however, because it played havoc with the foundation's public image and relations with Congress.

This is where my story begins. I came to NSF on July 1, 1975. Guyford Stever, director of NSF at the time, had been a long-term professor of physics at MIT and later president of Carnegie-Mellon University, as well as having served as an aide to Vannevar Bush during World War II. He had landed at Normandy on the second day of the invasion to seek out and investigate V-2 sites. The beach commander told his group that such a site had been liberated thirty miles up the road. When they arrived, they found the report had been a bit premature—the site was still occupied by the Germans. The German commander seized the opportunity to surrender, however, and all ended well. Newspaper reports established Stever as a national hero.

I was recruited by Stever to be the deputy director of NSF. I had never had any interest in administration as a university professor and frankly had a rather low regard for academic administrators—university presidents included. But the prospect of spending some time in Washington, D.C., was appealing to both my wife and me, particularly since our daughter was due to go off to college that fall. Why, one might ask, was I chosen by the people at NSF? I had a good relationship with the Kennedys; I had worked on Robert Kennedy's presidential campaign, and Senator Ted Kennedy was the chairman of NSF's Appropriations Committee. Even though I was a social scientist, I worked on mathematical problems, had been featured in *Life* magazine for having developed computer-based systems for education, and was a member of the National Academy of Sciences. I was not a hard scientist, but my pedigree was not too suspect. Guy Stever proved to be a persuasive recruiter, and so I joined NSF on a two-year leave from Stanford.

At this time considerable criticism was being directed toward science activities of all sorts. Ever since the publication of Rachel Carson's *Silent Spring* in the 1960s, there was a growing feeling abroad that the purity of science, as it had emerged from World War II, was not quite as pristine as it had seemed. This was immediately after the Vietnam War, and there were sizable cuts in science budgets; money was hard to come by, and scientists whose grants were not funded were critical of peer review and in turn of NSF. Proxmire was tapping into this public unease about science, and Congress followed his lead. During the winter before I came to NSF, two congressmen—John Conlan of

Arizona and Robert Bauman of Maryland—were particularly severe critics. They introduced a series of bills eliminating science education from NSF. Bauman had one bill that would have required every grant from NSF to be reviewed by Congress; it passed the House, and it was only thanks to the conference committee that the requirement was eliminated. The *Congressional Record* for that period is replete with speeches by senators and congressmen targeting NSF for criticism.

The criticism of science education programs became so intense that Stever wrote to Congress in March announcing his intention to establish an in-house group to review NSF's science education programs and to assess the criticisms that had been leveled at them. The group, which included some longtime insiders at NSF, was chaired by Bob Hughes, a new presidential appointee who served as one of the foundation's assistant directors. Hughes had a very heavy travel schedule, so his personal involvement in the study was limited.

The Hughes report was published a few days before I arrived at NSF, and it was the first thing I read. The report did not deal with the philosophical criticisms of NSF. Instead, it discussed NSF's business dealings and the appropriateness of its peer-review procedures as they applied to NSF curriculum projects. The report made a persuasive case that NSF had done its business in an orderly and thoroughly appropriate way, and I finished it convinced that the cloud of criticism hovering over NSF would soon be dispersed.

A few weeks later I was asked to testify on the Hill about the peer-review process as it was used throughout NSF. Director Stever was on a trip to Russia, so I went solo on my first appearance before Congress as a member of a federal agency. The chair of the committee was James Symington, son of the former senator Stuart Symington. He was sympathetic to NSF and many years later characterized his experience and the events associated with NSF's science education programs as comparable to his famous father's experience with Senator Joe McCarthy. Bauman and Conlan entered the room shortly after I started my testimony and immediately accused NSF of having produced a report that was "a pack of lies." We were deliberately misleading the Congress, they charged. I was stunned; there had never been criticism like this. When Stever returned from Russia, he joined me at the next peer-review hearing, where the same accusations were repeated. Finally, Stever responded in exasperation that we had done our very best to examine these matters, and if the Congress didn't think we had done a thorough job, it should call for a General Accounting Office [GAO] investigation. After the hearing ended, Symington suggested that such an investigation would surely silence the critics. Stever agreed, and so that summer the Congress initiated a GAO investigation.

The fall passed with hardly a mention of the GAO investigation. One Friday in early January, I received a call from Symington, who said he wanted to see me at three o'clock. When I arrived at his office, Symington was alone, with a stack of documents on his desk. One was the GAO report, sent first to him as the committee chairman. He told me to read the executive summary. My heart beat quickly as I scanned it. Then he handed me a press release, which he told me to read and change as I saw fit. The press release, he informed me, would be issued before I left his office. He wanted to be sure that Conlan and Bauman didn't get a jump on him and release the news before he did. The news, needless to say, was very bad indeed.

I got in touch with Stever as soon as I could. It was about six and he was in a tuxedo, about to go to a White House dinner for the president of France. We decided to assemble a group to examine the GAO report. Time was of the essence. I pulled together a small investigative team of people whom I had gotten to know at NSF and whom I trusted; none of them had served on the Hughes committee. By nine that evening we had sequestered the relevant files and were hard at work. We worked all night Friday, all day Saturday, and Saturday night as well. On Sunday morning I called Stever and went to his house in Georgetown. I explained to him that our investigation had made it clear the GAO report was not only correct, but it had merely scratched the surface. Matters were even worse than the GAO portrayed them. We spent several days in despair, struggling to decide what to do. My view was that we had to reveal everything as quickly as possible; others thought we should tough it out. A few days later, Stever met with Rice University president Norman Hackerman, chair of the National Science Board [NSB], the presidentially appointed oversight board of NSF. Stever explained the problem to him, and the two of them then asked me to outline a plan for dealing with the situation. I did so and was told that afternoon to proceed without delay—to get the whole story out, and quickly.

What did the GAO report say about our science curriculum projects? (1) NSF engaged in poor business practices. (2) It failed to do appropriate audits. (3) There were some inappropriate expenditures of funds. None of this was criminal, but it was clear that the foundation was doing a less than effective job. Many of these projects had gone on for more than six years with little effort to assess their quality or effectiveness. A particularly difficult criticism was that the curriculum programs often involved major commitments of funds—so much so that they had to go for final approval to the National Science Board. Yet the peer reviews sent to the NSB were redacted by program officers so that they were highly selective, emphasizing positive assessments and deleting negative ones.

Why did the Hughes group fail so badly? Hughes is a fine individual and a distinguished chemist who has been an important contributor to science policy. But he was a new presidential appointee with an incredibly heavy workload and travel schedule. He did not have time to monitor the committee's activities on a day-to-day basis or involve himself in a detailed analysis of the relevant documents. Unfortunately, some of the staff on the Hughes group conspired among themselves to cover up the problems. And how did Conlan and Bauman know what was going on? They had two people inside the NSF who were keeping them informed daily. A few years later, one of Conlan's aides remarked that they knew within hours after an NSF staff meeting exactly what had transpired.

NSF's response to the GAO report proved to be very effective. Our candor stunned the Congress and took the wind out of our critics' sails. We acknowledged the faults in our procedures, the questionable character of our business practices, and the inappropriateness of some of our expenditures. Two individuals were placed on administrative leave and one was later terminated. We restructured the science education programs, revised our policies, and recruited new leadership. There is an account of these changes in various NSF news releases and reports issued at that time.

We also changed the peer-review process throughout NSF. The program officers had, and still have, great flexibility. They solicit peer views for a given proposal and then use the information—as they judge appropriate—to decide whether or not to fund the project. Program officers should have that kind of decision-making authority, but there is also a need for oversight. Accordingly, we established an audit office that did random samples of peer reviews to ensure that they were being used appropriately.

In addition, we changed the procedure for soliciting peer reviews. Reviewers, in the past, had been told that applicants could request a copy of their review but that the review would be redacted to protect the identity of the reviewer. Redaction proved to be a serious problem in the GAO report and more generally throughout the foundation. Too many errors were made in the process (especially when many reviews had to be redacted), compromising the entire peer-review system. Accordingly, we told reviewers that in the future their reviews might be shared with applicants, and that they should write them in a way that protected their anonymity. Reviewers quickly adjusted to this procedure, and redaction was no longer necessary.

We also began to edit titles and abstracts of proposals to avoid the kinds of problems we had had with the *National Enquirer*. This proved to be necessary only on rare occasions, but the very idea created a stir in the academic community. "How dare you edit our work?" was a common reaction. I don't know whether they still do this at NSF, but in my day it was useful in preventing reporters from misrepresenting the true nature of a research project.

In the summer of 1976, Stever resigned to become science advisor to President Ford. Nixon had fired his science advisor, Ed David, and had abolished PSAC in 1973. He was unhappy with the academic community in part because of its anti–Vietnam

War activities. Nelson Rockefeller, Ford's vice president, believed that PSAC had played an important role in the past and should be reestablished, but with congressional legislation this time. That took a while, however, and in the summer of 1976 Stever became the director of the newly established Office of Science and Technology and I became acting director of NSF.

The next few months were possibly the most interesting of my life. I took steps to phase out the RANN [Research Applied to National Needs] program; in many respects it was a reasonably productive program, but its approach to the support of research was not appropriate for NSF and did not live up to our standards. I closed several regional offices, including one in San Francisco. I ordered a reduction in force—a RIF—a very unusual action in the federal government. These actions raised some hackles in Congress and OMB, but in my view I was cleaning house for the next director.

By the time Jimmy Carter was elected in 1976, I had the strong support of the National Science Board, whose membership included Frank Press, soon to be named the president's science advisor. The next thing I knew, I was nominated to be director of NSF. It was a move I had neither intended nor expected. Nor did I, with my social sciences background, quite fit the mold of an NSF director. Not long after my appointment, on a visit to Columbia University, I saw Dr. I. I. Rabi, an influential physicist during and after the Second World War. He told me he had heard only the best things about me and was so pleased I was going to be the director of NSF—and by the way, what field of physics was I in?

Perhaps my most important contribution as director was to recruit George Pimentel, from U.C. Berkeley, as deputy director.

George was a world-renowned chemist, whose death a few years ago was a great loss to science and to U.C. Berkeley. George and I worked well as a team and accomplished a great deal. Together we brought the business and administrative practices of NSF into the modern age. We expanded the behavioral and social sciences. We elevated engineering to the level of a full directorate. This pleased the engineering community, many of whose members were trying to get the foundation's name changed to "National Science and Engineering Foundation." We also established a research program in economics, focused on the role of R&D in stimulating economic growth; that field of research has prospered over the past twenty years and has led to an important development in economics known as "new growth theory."

It was also clear to us in the late 1970s that, while the nation's research universities were amazingly fruitful in producing new ideas, the process of transforming those ideas into applications—technology transfer—was not working as well as it should. We responded in several ways. NSF initiated the Industry-University Cooperative Research Program, a venture that was controversial in the 1970s but today is standard practice. In addition, we assembled a working group to address the federal policy that patents generated from government-supported research at universities should reside with the government. We conducted a series of policy studies that laid the groundwork for the passage in 1980 of the Bayh-Dole Act, which transferred patent rights to universities.

Those were the years when China, with the end of the Cultural Revolution, was beginning to open to the West. During my tenure as NSF director I negotiated and signed the first memorandum of understanding in history between the People's

Republic of China and the United States, an agreement for the exchange of scientists and scholars. Finally, I claim sole credit for establishing the Vannevar Bush Medal, awarded annually by the NSB to an individual who has made major contributions to the well-being of the science enterprise. As may be obvious, Bush stands tall in my eyes.

During my years as director, NSF received no Golden Fleece awards; Senator Proxmire, indeed, became a good friend to the foundation. In my last few weeks at NSF, Proxmire spoke at a seminar on biological methods of pest control. At the seminar he freely admitted that the study of the sex life of the screw-worm fly had been of major significance to progress in this important field.

I left NSF in July of 1980. Ronald Reagan was elected the following fall. He appointed as director of the budget David Stockman, whose first budget eliminated from NSF all science education activities (except graduate fellowships) and all of the social sciences. By the time the budget made its way through Congress, some of the social science activities had been reinstated, but at greatly reduced levels. A few years later, in an article in the *New York Times,* Stockman stated that he had made a mistake in eliminating these programs. On the other hand, he said, it was the kind of mistake he didn't mind making. But as the 1980s unfolded there was a renewed focus on science education throughout the country, and gradually NSF reintroduced and added programs in that area.

Congress always liked science education. One of NSF's problems was that most of the research it funded went to a relatively small group of universities; their concentration in a few large states complicated NSF's ability to gain broad support in

Congress. In science education, on the other hand, funds went to virtually all of the states. While I was director, we started a program to work with universities in states that received few NSF grants, giving them advice and assistance so that they could be more competitive in seeking grants. It was called Experimental Program to Stimulate Competitive Research, or EPSCoR, and is still in existence today. That is an interesting story all by itself, one that needs to be examined.

By 1992 the science education directorate was reestablished and the social sciences were viable, if not prospering, but clearly the reemergence of these two areas was influenced by earlier events. Some people argue that the foundation—shaped by these events—has been too cautious in its approach to science education and the social sciences.

Conlan lost the 1978 election. Bauman prospered throughout the 1970s—he was a leader on the floor of Congress and an important figure in the conservative movement. Everyone thought he would run for the Senate in 1982. Then the world came apart for him—he was arrested for sexually molesting a young boy. This story is told, with admirable candor, in his book *The Gentleman from Maryland: The Conscience of a Gay Conservative*. Once he had been arrested, his career was finished. He had been NSF's most severe, persistent, and unrelenting critic, charging that our efforts in science education served only to undermine the moral character of American children. Reading his book, I felt a certain sadness about what happened to him. But when I recall him across the witness table, my sadness is easier to bear.

The purpose of these remarks has been to give you a sense of the evolution of federal policy on science and science education in the postwar era, through the lens of my personal experience at NSF. The science enterprise during the postwar period needs to be interpreted from a variety of perspectives. Perhaps my experience will prove useful. Let me end as I began, with the hope that, if nothing else, these remarks may stimulate some young historians to take a fresh look at this fascinating era in the annals of American science.

NOTES

This paper was read at the Colloquium Series on the History of Science and Technology at the University of California at Berkeley, November 10, 1997, and published in the *Proceedings of the American Philosophical Society* vol. 143, no. 3 (September 1999). Reprinted with permission.

Remarks on Appointment as President of the University of California

August 1995

It is an honor to be selected the seventeenth president of the University of California. I come to the position with full knowledge of the enormous challenges facing the University. More importantly, I am inspired by the remarkable contributions that the University has made to the well-being of California. The people of California have created the finest public university in the world, and I am committed to maintaining its preeminence.

As we approach the twenty-first century, the University is more critical than ever to the economic vitality and social integrity of our society.

In economic terms, a society's wealth was once thought to be dependent upon its natural resources. Today, a society's wealth is the knowledge, creativity, and problem-solving abilities of its citizens. It is the University's responsibility—shared with the state's other public and private institutions—to enable Californians to achieve their full potential. We must continue to provide a challenging and rewarding education to our students so that they can compete in the global economy in which we now live.

In social terms, universities provide opportunities for students from widely varying backgrounds to come together and develop respect and understanding for each other. It is here that individual threads are woven together into a strong and resilient social fabric. We must continue to provide the highest-quality education to the full spectrum of qualified students. We must keep this commitment alive for our grandchildren and their grandchildren.

The University's ability to contribute to the economic and social well-being of California is dependent upon its capacity to create new knowledge through research. Not only do research and scholarship contribute to the excellence of our teaching programs, but they also yield large dividends in the form of new industries, new jobs, and an improved quality of life. We must do everything we can to maintain the vitality of the University's research programs.

In order to accomplish our mission, we will need to set clear priorities:

· First, the University must continue to attract and retain the best-qualified faculty and staff by remaining competitive with other leading universities.

· Second, to ensure that all students are afforded a quality education, the University must work with the California State University system and the California Community Colleges to maintain the promise of the Master Plan for Higher Education.

· Third, the University must provide greater assistance to elementary and secondary schools to give young people the best possible start in life.

· Fourth, the University must forge new research partnerships with industry and government to ensure California's continued economic progress.

· Finally, we must develop new management systems for the University that promote efficiency and guarantee accountability to the people of California.

Over the past several years, the Regents and President Peltason have held the University together through one of the most difficult periods in the history of California. More challenges are ahead. As we meet these challenges, I am convinced that the University will continue to provide rich dividends to the people of California, who have so generously supported the institution throughout its history. This institution has a special place in my heart, and I will do my utmost to ensure its future.

The University of California

The Future of the University of California: A Personal View

September 1998

The role of knowledge in transforming virtually every aspect of our world has moved research universities like the University of California to center stage of American life. More than any other institution in our society, research universities are on the cutting edge in producing the well-educated people who drive our economy and the new research ideas that keep it growing.

The tradition of research universities has been to value knowledge for its own sake. However, society's increasing need for applications of knowledge has placed new demands on these institutions, including the University of California, as we move into the twenty-first century. I want to discuss the organizational changes, goals, and initiatives U.C. needs to pursue to meet these demands and to sustain itself as a great university. These reflections do not cover all the issues of importance to the University. Instead, I am concentrating on a few of the trends that, in my judgment, will shape our future as a particular kind of university during a particular period in its history. I should emphasize that these are personal views. They have not been fully discussed with Regents, chancellors, faculty, or other members of the University community.

ASSUMPTIONS

I begin with some assumptions. The first assumption is that California will continue its thirty-eight-year commitment to the Master Plan for Higher Education. The combination of record numbers of students and constrained funding for higher education over the next two decades will test California's will to keep the Master Plan's promise of access, quality, and affordability. But although some details of the Master Plan may need to be altered to address new circumstances, its central idea—the concept of three public segments (the University of California, the California State University, and the Community Colleges) with different missions, admission standards, and responsibilities—should endure because it serves this state so well.

My second assumption is that the University of California's future is committed to the notion that we will remain a research university. And by the term *research university* I mean an institution in which the search for knowledge is at the center of everything we do. This does not mean a university in which research is carried out at the expense of undergraduate education. Rather, a university in which, in the words of a 1974 University of California mission statement, every responsibility is "shaped and bounded by the central and pervasive mission of discovering and advancing knowledge."

RESEARCH UNIVERSITIES IN
A KNOWLEDGE-BASED SOCIETY

For fifty years we have had a good understanding of the role of education as a driver of the economy, but it is only in the past ten to fifteen years that we have begun to fully understand the impact of research and development (R&D) on economic growth. A substantial literature on this subject has evolved, which has led to a development in economics called "new growth theory." This work is nicely summarized in a report by the Council of Economic Advisers: 50 percent of American economic growth since World War II has been the result of investments in research and development.[1] Obviously, the private sector is a major driver of R&D, but federally funded research in universities like U.C. also plays a key role. The literature also supports the conclusion that when investments in university research increase, there is (with an appropriate lag) a corresponding increase in private-sector investments.

No state in the country illustrates the connection between knowledge and wealth more vividly than California. Almost all of the industries in which California leads the world—biotechnology, software and computers, telecommunications, multimedia, semiconductors, environmental technologies—were born of university-based research. Hewlett-Packard, one of the top ten exporter companies in the United States, estimates that over half its revenue comes from products that were developed within the past two years. More and more of these products are emerging from work done at universities.

Ensuring strong economic growth has implications beyond simple dollars and cents. The state and the nation face tremendous problems—deteriorating inner cities, homelessness, degradation of the environment, the prospect of a huge number of Baby Boomers retiring with a far smaller workforce to support them in their retirement. How are we going to deal with these problems? There is only one way—we must have substantial economic growth. This requires investments in university-based research and a highly educated workforce. The link between California's success and the success of its universities is clear and direct.

Even as research universities are being called on to contribute more to economic vitality, they are being transformed by a revolution they themselves helped create. The way learning takes place—the interaction between teacher and student—has not varied much since the time of Plato's Academy over two thousand years ago. But today, computer and communication technologies are creating a dramatically different environment.

Videoconferencing, interactive instruction via the Internet, and various forms of computer-assisted learning are transforming the educational process throughout the University of California. There are many examples, but one of the most exciting is the recently established California Digital Library (CDL).[2] This is a virtual library that will make U.C.'s digital collections—not just books but works of art as well—available via computer to U.C. faculty and students. Ultimately, the CDL is intended to be California's library, open to all the citizens of this state. We will accomplish this goal through a partnership with the California State Library and California library leaders to employ the CDL as the primary means of making digital library services available throughout California.

The California Digital Library illustrates how learning is beginning to transcend the conventional limits of time and space that have bound universities to a particular place and a particular schedule. The term *lifelong learning* takes on new meaning in light of the capacity of these technologies to reach people beyond the doors of our campuses, in their homes, offices, and community centers.

What these two phenomena—society's growing dependence on knowledge and the technological revolution in education—will ultimately mean for the organization and role of universities is a topic we have barely begun to understand. But it is clear that we need to look at the university anew in light of both the demands and the possibilities of a knowledge-based society.

U.C. AS A COLLECTION OF
TEN RESEARCH UNIVERSITIES

Such a knowledge-based society requires a university sufficiently large in scope to span the map of knowledge but flexible enough to respond to the economy's shifting demands for educated people and the research necessary to keep productivity growing. What does this suggest for our vision of the University?

We envision U.C. as a collection of ten research universities—as a single but not a monolithic institution of ten campuses—not all identical and not all moving toward the same template. Just as Princeton and the University of Michigan are both research universities but clearly different in size, in the array of academic disciplines, and in the makeup of their professional schools, so the University of California's campuses can be seen as variations on a single theme, each pursuing excellence in different ways.

What are the implications for the future of viewing U.C. from this perspective?

· Each campus will be differentiated, even at the level of individual disciplines. All campuses will have mathematics and history, for example, but not every subfield. This is consistent with the philosophy that guided the creation of three new U.C. campuses in the 1960s, each distinctive in academic emphases, organization, and physical design. The idea was not to replicate Berkeley or UCLA but to develop new university options for the people of California. And the fiscal reasons are clear: prospects for state support are such that we cannot afford to offer the complete array of disciplines and subdisciplines, graduate and undergraduate courses, at every campus.

· There will be greater decentralization of authority from the Office of the President to the campuses. This, too, is consistent with trends in the University's development since the late 1950s. At the same time, the Office of the President must play a leadership and coordinating role, as, for example, ensuring that all campuses comply with University-wide policy and regulations, evaluating the quality of programs system-wide, and determining which fields to emphasize at which campuses. An example of the Office of the President's role in setting system-wide academic priorities is U.C.'s engineering initiative. Business leaders have expressed their concern that unless this state produces more engineers, California companies cannot remain competitive. Our own studies have substantiated this concern. In response, the Office of the President initiated a plan to increase significantly undergraduate and graduate enrollment in engineering and computer science programs across the U.C. system.

· The reciprocal of greater decentralization is greater account-ability. Campuses will be held responsible for fulfilling campus and University-wide priorities, while the Office of the President will concentrate on outcomes and monitoring accountability.

· The ratio of graduate to undergraduate students will vary from campus to campus, department to department, discipline to discipline. Traditionally, this ratio has been driven more by the teaching and research needs of faculty than by the market-place. In the future the marketplace will be a principal deter-miner of how many doctoral students we produce in various fields.[3] Over the past several years, we have been modifying our graduate enrollments in various disciplines as a function of stu-dent demand, market demand, societal need, and our ability to support graduate students. I do not mean to imply that the University's current graduate enrollments are too high; in fact, the opposite is the case. The proportion of graduate students at the University has declined from 29.4 percent in 1960 to 17.8 percent today. To put these figures into perspective, it is useful to look at graduate enrollments at the eight universities with which U.C. compares itself for faculty salary purposes. As of 1993, the percentage of graduate and professional students at U.C.'s public comparison institutions averaged 30 percent; the average for our private comparison institutions was 52.8 per-cent. It is clear that, at less than 18 percent, U.C.'s graduate enrollments are far too low.

· To help the University maintain both quality and access, campuses have been given greater flexibility in how they use re-sources. Campuses have freedom to set campus priorities and deploy resources, but they also have to enter into an agreement with the Office of the President that reflects both University-wide and campus-specific expectations.

GOALS AND INITIATIVES

The purpose of these changes is to organize the University to carry out its missions of teaching, research, and public service in ways that capitalize on its strengths and that respond to society's demands for new knowledge and well-educated people. Meeting those demands will require that we pursue the following goals and initiatives:

· The quality of the entire University enterprise depends on the quality of its faculty. U.C.'s ability to recruit and retain the very best scholars and scientists is fundamental to its capacity to remain a great university.

· The University must be prepared to educate its share of the estimated 538,000 new students seeking a college or university education between 1994 and 2005—an increase in enrollment demand of 31 percent for California higher education generally. According to the California Education Round Table, these figures translate to an enrollment growth rate two and a half times that expected for the nation as a whole. The shorthand term for this phenomenon is Tidal Wave II, and it is surely the single most significant issue facing higher education in this state. We estimate that U.C. will grow by about 45,000 students between now and the year 2010, with almost half of that expansion occurring before 2005. U.C.'s planned tenth campus in Merced, which will open its doors in 2005, will help accommodate some of this demand.

· U.C. plays a critical role in research as it affects the economic vitality of California. U.C. will not become a "job shop" for industry and will not compromise the quality, independence, or breadth of its research enterprise. What we will do is explore new forms of collaboration with industry to bring U.C.'s tremendous intellectual resources to bear on stimulating productivity and economic growth. The U.C. Industry-University Cooperative Research program is an important step toward that goal. Its aim is to build partnerships with industry to mine promising research areas for new products and processes that will create jobs and prosperity for California. The doubling (from 12 to 24 percent) of the tax credit industries receive for investing in university research makes this an especially auspicious time to expand research partnerships with industry. The tax credit encourages more industry investment in R&D generally; U.C.'s cooperative research program targets specific, next-generation research in areas of California's greatest strength and opportunity. Together, they offer an historic opportunity to forge a strategy for California's economic preeminence into the next century.

· We must maintain U.C.'s world leadership in the application of digital technology to problems of instruction. An incredible array of instructional technologies has been developed on each of our campuses, and we must continue to be a leader in this field. We want to be sure, too, that the K-12 schools are on the cutting edge of instructional technology. Toward this goal, we have mounted a system-wide initiative called U.C. Nexus to promote a statewide partnership between U.C. and the K-12 schools in encouraging high-quality teaching and learning through instructional technology. U.C.'s role will be to help train and support teachers in the use of computers for instruction and to help develop K-12 curricula.

· The University will explore new paths to teaching and learning. Among these paths will be closer linkages between the campuses and University Extension. The emergence of new professions, the restructuring of the workplace, and the transition to an information-based economy are requiring individuals to renew skills throughout their lifetimes. This means that today, U.C. Extension is more important than ever: it offers continuing education to over five hundred thousand Californians annually, at no cost to the state, and there can be no question about the excellence of its contributions to educating California's workforce. But I believe our view of Extension's potential has not been broad enough, and that this potential can be best realized by integrating Extension more closely into the University as a whole. A new initiative called the Master of Advanced Study is a step in that direction. This program will offer professional education and liberal studies beyond the bachelor's degree at times and places that are convenient for working adults. Courses will be offered by U.C. academic departments in partnership with University Extension, and the curriculum will be supervised by regular faculty members.

· Every university worthy of the name embraces a diversity of thought and opinion. As a public university in one of the most diverse states in the nation, the University of California has the further obligation of reflecting the mix of the state's population in the mix of its students, faculty, and staff. Both forms of diversity—a wide range of intellectual perspectives and a broad representation of California's population—are indispensable to our mission as a public university.

In enacting new policies on graduate and undergraduate admissions in July 1995, the Regents called for a task force on outreach to help establish new paths to diversity. The Outreach Task Force finished its work last year, and the Regents approved its recommendations. To implement the task force's report, we have launched a major initiative called the Outreach Action Plan. We are committed to doubling our investment in outreach from 60 to 120 million dollars a year. At the heart of the plan is a renewed partnership between the University and the K-12 schools. Implementation of the Outreach Action Plan is among the University's highest priorities.

SCHOLARSHIP AND TEACHING IN A RESEARCH UNIVERSITY

The most important single contribution we can make to California—the one from which all others flow—is to keep the University intellectually vital. To accomplish this, we need a broad range of intellectual activity both in and across disciplines. Research is constantly exploring the boundaries between what we know and what we do not know. Sometimes the pace of discovery is greater in one discipline or era than in another, as in the blossoming of art in fifteenth-century Florence or the revolution in physics early in this century. But the exploration of all domains of knowledge is the daily business of the University. As one scholar has put it, lyric poetry and magnetic resonance imagery may be very different, but both are ways of giving us access to information that would be otherwise inaccessible. We do not expect every faculty member to win a Pulitzer Prize or become a Nobel laureate. We do expect every faculty member to be engaged in innovative and intellectually challenging work.

And part of that innovative and intellectually challenging work is educating undergraduates. As a research university—not a research institute—we regard students as indispensable to everything we are and aspire to be. Given public perceptions about the academic performance of American students and the problems of American schools, it may come as a surprise to some that the students who enroll in the University today are the best prepared in history. These students are entrusted to us during what is, for many of them, one of the most critical and intellectually passionate periods of their lives. The process of education should help them focus their curiosity and enthusiasm and bring them into contact with the rigor and objectivity that are essential to the life of the mind. A research university—full of bright individuals with their own passionate commitments to learning—is a wonderful place in which to pursue such an education.

Much has been made in recent years of the notion of a core curriculum—a specific body of knowledge every student should master. Everyone has a different prescription for what the core curriculum should include. I am less committed to a core set of ideas. Rather, I prefer the Aristotelian approach that stresses knowledge of many areas and deep experience in at least one. My conclusion after many years on the San Diego campus—where five undergraduate colleges offer five core curricula, all different, all rigorous, all intellectually demanding—is that there are many equally valid curricular paths to intellectual growth.

What is ultimately going to matter to students when their college years are over is not the particular books they read or the specific curriculum they followed but the cognitive skills they acquired. An in-depth knowledge of a particular subject is essential to knowing how to do something—to make a life's work. To master knowledge in one domain is also to master the grammar of learning, the intellectual and problem-solving skills that can be applied to learning virtually anything. Every student who possesses this grammar has the foundation on which future learning can be built.

In recent years there have been thoughtful dialogues in the University of California about undergraduate education, with impressive results. Our undergraduates have the opportunity to engage in supervised research and to learn in an environment of discovery from professors who are on the cutting edge of new developments. Those students who can thrive on its demands find that education at U.C. offers unrivaled opportunities for learning. Students graduating from U.C. leave with a superb intellectual foundation, and they make a contribution to this state precisely because they are so well educated.

One of the criticisms often leveled at research universities is that they do not adequately reward the faculty for excellent teaching. The report of U.C.'s University-wide Task Force on Faculty Rewards emphasized the importance of recognizing "the scholarship of integration, application, and teaching" as well as "the scholarship of discovery."[4] Furthermore, academic career rhythms are not uniform, nor is the relationship between research and teaching the same in different disciplines.[5] The task force recommended that criteria for advancement be flexible in allowing faculty to shift emphases on teaching and research over the course of their careers. We need this kind of flexibility not just for the sake of our faculty but also for our students, who deserve exceptional teachers and teaching.

CONCLUDING REMARKS

The University of California is an 11.5 billion-dollar-a-year enterprise. The State of California contributes about 2 billion dollars of that 11.5 billion dollars, which means that for every dollar the state provides, we generate almost five dollars in other funds. One reason is that U.C. is a major recipient of federal research dollars, attracting over 10 percent of all federal funds spent on research in American universities.

Because of its extraordinary size and unparalleled strengths in teaching, research, and public service, the University of California is a major contributor to the well-being of the state and the nation. The University's future, therefore, matters far beyond our campuses and research stations. What more can we say about where U.C. is headed?

Externally, the University is moving toward closer integration with society because of the tremendous potential of knowledge to leverage economic growth and to improve the quality of life for Californians. Internally, the University is moving toward greater autonomy for individual campuses and new ways of providing education and performing research. Another way to put it is that the future is drawing the University of California in two seemingly contradictory directions. One direction is toward greater diversity and decentralization as a strategy to use our resources most effectively. The other direction is toward greater unity as a result of the revolution wrought by the marriage of computers and telecommunication, which is opening up new modes of learning and expanding exponentially the boundaries of the university.

The future of the University depends on our success in balancing the tensions and opportunities inherent in a ten-campus enterprise. This means realizing the possibilities of our unity as well as our diversity. In the past, thanks to a fortunate combination of leadership, circumstances, and determination, U.C. has been one of the most successful balancing acts in higher education. Our responsibilities in today's knowledge-based society require us to embrace the future with realism, intelligence, and a clear sense of the University of California's destiny as this nation's preeminent example of that vigorous American hybrid, the research university.

NOTES

This paper is based on a presentation made to the Council of Chancellors of the University of California in April 1996.

1. The Council of Economic Advisers, "Supporting Research and Development to Promote Economic Growth: The Federal Government's Role," October 1995. Available at www.clintonlibrary.gov/archivesearch.html.

2. "California's Library without Limits," *San Diego Union-Tribune,* October 14, 1997.

3. See "The Numbers Game and Graduate Education," in this volume.

4. University of California Office of the President, "Report of the Universitywide Task Force on Faculty Rewards," June 26, 1991.

5. See Richard C. Atkinson and Donald Tuzin, "Equilibrium in the Research University," *Change,* May–June 1992.

The Role of the
President of the University

December 1997

The 1868 Organic Act proclaimed that the University of California would be led by a "President of the several Faculties . . . [who would also be] the executive head of the institution in all its departments." Despite this sweeping description of the president's powers, the office carried academic but little administrative authority in the early days of the University. In 1890, for example, it took a special amendment to the Regents' Bylaws to give the president authority "to employ, dismiss, and regulate the duties of janitors."[1] As late as 1901, the Regents were still giving individual consideration to each request for replacement of a lost diploma. It was not until the administration of Benjamin Ide Wheeler (1899–1920) that the president truly became, in fact as well as in theory, the chief executive officer of the University.

By the late 1950s, however, it was clear that the University had outgrown the ability of any one person to administer. The enormous Baby Boom generation was coming of college age, and the University was planning the expansion of its existing campuses and the creation of three new ones at La Jolla, Irvine, and Santa Cruz. Recognizing that these new circumstances required new ways of organizing the University, the Regents and the president embarked on a course of decentralizing authority and responsibility to the individual campuses and chancellors. The far-reaching changes they instituted created the University of California as we know it today: a federated system of ten research universities, each seeking excellence in its own way but unified by common standards for the admission of students, the appointment and promotion of faculty, and the approval of academic programs, and united in its pursuit of the common goals of educating students, discovering and creating knowledge, and serving the people of California. As a result, the University of California is more than the sum of its individual campuses. It is a vast educational enterprise created and sustained by California's citizens.

Today the University is an eleven-billion-dollar organization that stretches the length and breadth of California, encompassing ten campuses—each with its own chancellor—166,000 undergraduate and graduate students, nearly 400,000 students enrolled in University Extension, 7,000 faculty, nearly 150,000 employees, and almost 850,000 living alumni. The president is responsible for the overall policy direction of the University and shares authority for its operation with the faculty, to whom the Regents have delegated primary responsibility for educational policy, and with the chancellors, each of whom reports to the president but has broad responsibility for the day-to-day management of his or her campus.

The president has many duties within this multicampus system; the Standing Orders of the Regents list forty separate responsibilities. But in my judgment the most important boil down to the following:

· The president is responsible for recommending to the Regents the appointment of chancellors and for conducting the five-year reviews of their performance. Probably no other presidential responsibility has as dramatic and lasting an influence on the character, quality, and success of the University of California.

· The president is responsible for recommending new policy directions to the Regents. Many issues and decisions facing the University involve only one campus and are entirely within the purview of the chancellor and the campus community. Many other issues cut across campuses and demand a University-wide perspective and action, and it is on these issues that the president is expected to lead. This cannot be done successfully without widespread consultation among Regents, faculty, staff, students, and anyone else who has something to contribute and a stake in the outcome. Recent examples are the establishment of a tenth U.C. campus and the decision to offer domestic-partner health benefits.

· The president is responsible for preparing and managing the budget of the University and for assuring the Regents, the governor and the legislature, and the public that the University is exercising good stewardship of the public funds entrusted to its care. The Office of the President, through the University Auditor, sets University-wide policies and professional standards in this area, monitors audit activities throughout the system, and reports to the Regents on these activities. It is also important to note that our stewardship responsibilities are not limited only to the use of public funds—in a larger sense, the University must also demonstrate that it is worthy of the loyalty, support, and confidence the people of California have given it over many years.

· Similarly, the president is responsible for ensuring the quality of the University's academic programs systemwide, for helping to shape decisions about which academic fields to emphasize at which campuses, for seeing that all campuses comply with University-wide policy and regulations, and for overseeing the creation of new campuses. When things go right, this monitoring and oversight role is virtually invisible to the world outside the University's doors. When they go wrong, the president is front and center in the public spotlight. Despite U.C.'s decentralized character and the broad campus authority delegated to the chancellors, the president bears ultimate responsibility for the University—and is regularly and forcefully reminded of that fact by unhappy officials, irate citizens, and, on occasion, dissatisfied students.

· Although the president is not the only person who represents U.C., he or she is the only person who can speak on behalf of the entire University. Each chancellor speaks for his or her campus; the faculty, on behalf of the academic interests of the University; students, staff, and alumni, on behalf of their constituencies; the Regents, on broad questions of policy. The president is the bridge to each and all of these. This is a humbling, sobering, and occasionally alarming thought for the occupant of the president's office. And it suggests a critical dimension of the president's role that no delegation of authority or job description can capture. The president must see that the various members of the University's huge extended family are talking to each other, working with each other, and headed in roughly the same direction. This is neither easy nor always achievable, especially in times of controversy and conflict. But it is essential.

As the seventeenth president of this great university, I am following in the footsteps of an impressive company of academic leaders: Henry Durant, Daniel Coit Gilman, Benjamin Ide Wheeler, Robert Gordon Sproul, and Clark Kerr, to mention a few. The presidency has changed as the University has grown and prospered. It remains, however, the pivotal influence for managing and supporting one of the most distinguished and productive university systems in the world.

Finally, let me say that one of my goals as president is to see that the educational experience of U.C.'s students is as good as we can make it. I believe that U.C. offers an undergraduate and graduate education second to none, but only because the quality of that education is a paramount concern not only to me but also to the chancellors and the faculty. As well it should be. Much has changed since U.C. burst on the scene in 1868 with a student body of thirty-eight and a faculty of ten, but students remain now, as they were then, the lifeblood of the University.

NOTES

This piece was published in U.C. student newspapers in December 1997.

1. Verne A. Stadtman, ed., *The Centennial Record of the University of California* (Berkeley: University of California, 1967).

Robert Gordon Sproul

November 1999

Robert Gordon Sproul graduated from the University of California, Berkeley, in the same class as his friend Earl Warren and, like Warren, was destined to become a shaper of events in twentieth-century California. But unlike Warren, the future governor and Supreme Court justice, Sproul chose to devote his prodigious energies to a single institution—the University of California.

In 1914, after a year working for the city of Oakland as an efficiency engineer following his college graduation, Sproul joined the U.C. comptroller's office in Berkeley. He would spend the next forty-four years with the University, twenty-eight of them as its president.

He began his career under the great university builder Benjamin Ide Wheeler, whose leadership had made U.C. Berkeley the largest and one of the best research universities in the country. With the opening in 1919 of the Southern Branch—later known as UCLA—California also became home to the nation's first multicampus system.

Sproul was influenced by Wheeler's grand vision of a public university that would not only educate California's leaders but involve itself productively in the economic and social life of the state. Sproul was a political realist, however, who tempered his aspirations for U.C. with a keen sense of the possible. As comptroller, he learned the political ropes firsthand, defending the University's budget requests before the legislature. His commanding voice, photographic memory, and political deftness made him an immediate success in the halls of Sacramento and far beyond.

Sproul needed these skills and more when the U.C. Regents chose him to head the system in 1930. The nation was plunging into the Depression, and California was hard hit. Sproul traveled constantly to garner the financial and political support of alumni, farmers, community groups, and business interests.

In 1933, after agreeing to draconian budget cuts, the University was threatened with a further two-million-dollar reduction proposed by the Assembly Ways and Means Committee. Sproul broadcast a radio plea that the University be exempted from this additional cut. His eloquence stimulated an outpouring of letters and telegrams to the legislature, many of them prompted by students who wrote home to their parents. The University was spared.

Despite the hard times, demand for higher education was growing, and many legislators were inclined to establish more four-year colleges, or to expand existing community colleges into four-year institutions. Sproul's position was both sensible and self-interested. He persuaded the legislature to mandate a study of California higher education that had two important outcomes—a check on the regional college movement and the establishment of the State Council for Educational Planning and Coordination, one of the first attempts in California history to develop strategies for the orderly growth of the state's colleges and universities.

Even before becoming president, Sproul recognized that the center of the state's political gravity would ultimately shift to the south, and that the Southern Branch must grow into a full-fledged U.C. campus to meet the needs of the burgeoning Los Angeles region. He enthusiastically supported the development of UCLA.

By the time he left office in 1958, UCLA was a distinguished university recognized worldwide for the excellence of its programs. And the University of California, with six campuses from Davis to Los Angeles, was poised for the amazing expansion of the 1960s, when U.C. added three more campuses and educated the Baby Boom generation.

Sproul was not trained as an academic and in that sense differed from most university presidents. But he believed absolutely in the ideal of the land-grant university involved in service to society, and he articulated it brilliantly. He inherited a university that, even in 1930, was unmatched in the variety of its academic programs, the quality and relevance of its research to California's economy, and its commitment to serve the needs of a state in the throes of major economic transition. But it took his enormous gifts as a leader to rally Californians to secure the financial and political support that U.C. needed to become a world-renowned multicampus system.

He was courted by politicians and businesspeople, offered distinguished academic positions and lucrative nonacademic jobs, urged to run for governor, senator, and even president of the United States. He would have none of it. He was president of the University of California, and that was all he wanted.

In a tribute honoring Sproul's twenty-fifth anniversary in office, a faculty member summed it up: "Doubtless God could have made a better president, but doubtless God never did."

NOTES

This article was published in the *California Journal,* November 1999. Copyright held by Department of Special Collections and University Archives, the Library California State University, Sacramento. Sources: George A. Pettitt, *Twenty-eight Years in the Life of a University President* (Berkeley: University of California Press, 1966), and Verne A. Stadtman, *The University of California, 1868–1968* (New York: McGraw Hill, 1970).

Tradition at the University of California

Regents' Dinner
September 1998

Let me add my welcome to the one you've already received from the chairman of the Board of Regents. A special welcome to the leaders of the business community who are joining us this evening. You are all individuals who have made important contributions to the University of California and to your communities, and this is an opportunity to thank you and to get to know you a little better.

These are good times for the University of California. Although we face some major challenges—among them ensuring diversity in a post–Proposition 209 world—it is clear that U.C. is a remarkably strong institution. We have a superb faculty. The quality of our students is better than at any point in our history. Our research programs are outstanding and highly competitive; U.C.'s share of federal contract and grant funds is greater than it has ever been.

Despite a decade that has brought California more deficits than surpluses, we have maintained the quality of the University.

Our most recent budget from the State of California provides for a 15.6 percent increase, the largest in many years. This reflects not only California's returning economic vigor but also the fact that the governor, the legislature, and the public believe that U.C. contributes to the quality of life in this state. And apparently our alumni and friends agree: for the fourth year in a row, private giving reached record levels.

Tonight, I want to talk briefly about one of the important contributors to U.C.'s success: the traditions that have made this a distinguished institution and that have sustained us in good times and in bad. I spoke recently about this topic to the members of the Order of the Golden Bear on the Berkeley campus, on the occasion of my initiation into that body. The Order of the Golden Bear is first and foremost a student organization, although over the years it has come to include some faculty, alumni, and staff among its members. It is itself one of U.C.'s wonderful traditions, having been founded by President Benjamin Ide Wheeler in 1900.

U.C. was still a young institution in 1900, and Wheeler had high ambitions and a strong commitment to quality. He was one of the presidents who put U.C. on the road to international recognition. Yet I doubt that Wheeler, or anyone else in 1900, could have imagined the size, scope, and significance U.C. would attain a century later. It would be interesting, from today's perspective, to speculate on the significance U.C. will have one hundred years hence.

I told the members of the Order that though there are many University traditions—Charter Day, the U.C. hymn, and so forth—I would focus on three.

The first tradition is free speech—the proposition that a university must be an open marketplace for ideas. We stuttered occasionally along the way, especially during the loyalty-oath controversy in the 1950s, but with few exceptions U.C. has lived by the highest standards in this domain.

The second tradition is shared governance—the idea that responsibility for the University is a partnership among faculty, administration, and Regents. It is no accident that the University of California's first real steps toward greatness coincided with the introduction of shared governance over seventy-five years ago. It has played a pivotal role in the University's history and in the history of American higher education. In embracing shared governance, U.C. pioneered a path that other universities were to follow. Most American universities now agree on the importance of shared governance, even though the specific processes and mechanisms may vary from those at the University of California.

The third tradition is academic excellence. Among universities generally, U.C.'s level of quality is unusual. Among public universities, it is unique. And that quality exists across an entire system of nine (soon to be ten) campuses, not just one or two. I am convinced that during the terrible budget years of the early 1990s, the University's tradition of excellence was a powerful factor in the loyalty displayed by so many distinguished faculty members who could easily have gone elsewhere but chose to stay.

Further, U.C.'s excellence is reflected in the three national laboratories we manage for the Department of Energy. Our stewardship of the national laboratories was and is a tremendous contribution to the security of this nation. The outcome of the cold war was dependent on the quality of supervision we provided, the people we attracted, and the programs we mounted, all of which have contributed to world peace. As the Regents know from reports by the chairman of the President's Council on the Department of Energy Laboratories, U.C.'s stewardship has been of critical importance. It allows the laboratories to maintain the breadth and independence of their R&D activities, as the research agendas of federal agencies tend to change on short time scales. It also permits them to attract the best scientists and engineers because of the greater freedom of inquiry our management fosters.

These three traditions—freedom of speech, shared governance, and academic excellence—are the bedrock on which the University of California is built. They have played an indispensable role in making U.C. admired and respected throughout the world. No matter where I go, I find that the University's reputation has gone before me.

Last week my travels took me to Washington, D.C., where I participated in the unveiling of a report by the Council on Competitiveness. The Council on Competitiveness is composed of 140 leaders from universities and the corporate and labor sectors who are committed to working together on a national action agenda to keep the United States competitive in today's knowledge-based economy. The council's report, "Going Global," includes case studies of five industries, based on interviews with CEOs about the current state of U.S. innovation and the factors essential to maintaining it.[1] There were variations among the different industries in terms of investment patterns, personnel structures, and research needs. But there were also four common themes that related to universities:

· All the CEOs surveyed are very concerned about meeting industry's needs for educated people, in terms of the quality of undergraduates generally and especially engineering and computer-science students. This country faces a tremendous shortfall of engineers, computer scientists, and other specialists. Together, universities in the United States graduated twenty-five thousand majors in computer science last year—down 25 percent from just ten years ago. We are having trouble drawing students into these critical fields. I was pleased to report that U.C. has made a commitment to expand engineering enrollments by 40 percent over the next eight years, and even more pleased to report that our faculty has responded so positively. California has the most knowledge-intensive economy in the world, and expanding the supply of scientists and engineers is a contribution to the state's competitiveness that U.C. is uniquely qualified to make.

· The CEOs surveyed clearly recognized the key significance of university research. Every industry pointed to its dependence on university research to pursue its opportunities in innovation. This is a turnaround from attitudes fifteen years ago, when so many complained that the country would be better served if research universities would concentrate exclusively on undergraduate teaching. Today, the role of the research university as a driver of economic growth is well understood by CEOs, governors, and legislators around the country, perhaps especially here in California.

· Another strong theme was the immense value of cooperation between universities and industry and the need for closer collaboration. U.C. has been extremely active in these efforts. The Regents are well aware of the Industry-University Cooperative

Research Program, which has received special funding from the legislature for the past several years. But there are many other instances of cooperative efforts throughout the University. Clearly, the most long-standing are in the area of agriculture and natural resources, where numerous well-established cooperative programs exist. I have considered doing a crosscut on U.C.'s budget to get a better estimate of all university-industry activities, but it would be a lengthy undertaking because there are so many different places where these exchanges occur. There is no question that we are in a leadership role in the area of cooperative research with industry.

· CEOs were unanimous in emphasizing the importance of K-12 education and the critical importance of the early years—points that were also made forcefully during the report on outreach at today's Regents' meeting. When the Regents adopted SP-1, they made a clear commitment to focus on diversity, to use means other than race to ensure that the University reflects California's diverse society. The responsibility of the Outreach Task Force mandated by SP-1 was to examine and rethink our current programs and to create a strategy for ensuring U.C.'s diversity in today's post–Proposition 209 era. The task force estimated that to make real progress, we would need to double our expenditures on outreach from 60 million dollars a year to 120 million dollars within five years. I enthusiastically agreed to that goal, though not without some concern about our ability to achieve it. But I am pleased to report that we have had strong support for our programs from the private sector, the governor, and the legislature, and as a result we will be spending about 141 million dollars next year on outreach—well ahead of our five-year schedule.

These are exciting times in which to be president of the University of California. I am proud of what we have accomplished throughout this century and believe there are many opportunities to contribute even more in the next century. Among public universities, we have played a special role in maintaining quality. We must continue to focus on that U.C. tradition of excellence as we move into the next century. It is our quality—our outstanding instructional programs, research, and faculty—that makes us so important to the state and the nation.

Thank you for all you do on behalf of the University of California. Your involvement has contributed to the greatness of this institution and in turn to the well-being of all Californians.

NOTES

1. "Going Global: The New Shape of American Innovation," available at www.compete.org.

Diversity: Not There Yet

April 2003

In the weeks leading up to the Supreme Court's hearing on affirmative action, the public University of California system was depicted alternately as a dramatic success or a dismal failure in its efforts to enroll Latino and African American students after the elimination of race and ethnicity as factors in student admissions.[1]

The truth lies somewhere in between. But as a university president who took office just after the decision in California to disallow consideration of race and ethnicity in University admissions—and as one who retires a few months from now—I have concluded that we are still not doing a good enough job of providing access for the full diversity of students in our state.

California is a rapidly diversifying society. In 1990, 34 percent of the state's public school students were Latinos; in 2000, the figure was 43 percent; and by 2010, it is projected to be 52 percent. Against this backdrop of stunning demographic change stands a public school system characterized by vast disparities in educational opportunity. There are many excellent public high schools, each of which sends dozens of graduates to the U.C. system each year. Meanwhile, there are many schools that send hardly any students to U.C.

The impact of educational disadvantage is evident in students' eligibility rates for the U.C. system, which are defined by high school grades and standardized-test scores. The most recent study found that 30 percent of Asian American students in California and 13 percent of white students met U.C. eligibility requirements; the figure was a disheartening 4 percent for Latinos and 3 percent for African Americans.

The University always has sought to maintain the highest possible academic standards, while providing the broadest possible access to California students. We have pursued both excellence and diversity because we believe they are inextricably linked, and because we know that an institution that ignores either of them runs the risk of becoming irrelevant in a state with the knowledge-based economy and tremendously varied population of California.

The U.C. system in an earlier period took account of race and ethnicity in its admissions process. Latino, African American, and Native American applicants were identified as "underrepresented minority" students, reflecting these groups' low eligibility rates traditionally, and that factor was taken into account in the admissions process. But a contentious vote of the Board of Regents in 1995, followed by a statewide initiative passed by California voters in 1996, ended that practice.

In its place, U.C. launched a greatly intensified program of outreach to public schools, working in partnership to improve academic performance and college eligibility in schools that traditionally sent few students to U.C. We took on a vastly expanded role in providing professional development for K-12 teachers. And we made changes in our admissions process—such as granting U.C. eligibility to the top 4 percent of students in every California high school—that, while not aimed specifically at diversity, have had the effect of expanding U.C. access for educationally disadvantaged students.

What have been the results for underrepresented minority students? In some respects, the story is encouraging. After an initial drop, these students have represented an increasing proportion of the U.C. entering class in each of the past four years. This year the absolute number of underrepresented minority freshmen at U.C. campuses exceeds the number enrolled before race and ethnicity were eliminated as admissions considerations.

But the story is troubling in at least two respects. First, the proportions of underrepresented minority students at U.C.'s more selective campuses—particularly U.C. Berkeley and UCLA—remain far below their previous levels. Second, the gap between the percentage of underrepresented minority students in the California graduating high school class and the percentage in the U.C. freshman class has widened appreciably.

In 1995, 38 percent of California public high school graduates were underrepresented minority students, as were 21 percent of U.C. freshmen—a gap of 17 percentage points. In 2002, however, the figures were 42 percent in the statewide high school graduating class and 18 percent in the U.C. freshman class—a gap of 24 percentage points. Gains in minority admissions at U.C. are not closing this gap, because the diversity of the California high school population continues to grow.

What we do about this is a source of real concern. We must continue our efforts to help close the achievement gap in the public schools. We must continue refining our admissions policies to ensure that they reward high achievement and yet recognize that high achievement can be demonstrated in different ways in different educational settings.

But I offer California as a cautionary tale to the rest of the nation. Our experience to date shows that if race cannot be factored into admissions decisions at all, the ethnic diversity of an elite public institution such as the University of California may fall well behind that of the state it serves. And that is something that should trouble us all.

NOTES

This opinion piece was published in the *Washington Post* April 20, 2003. © 2003 The Washington Post Company.

1. The cases under consideration by the Supreme Court, *Gratz v. Bollinger* and *Grutter v. Bollinger,* involved admissions practices at the University of Michigan. In June 2003, the Supreme Court ruled that race could be considered as one of a number of factors in admitting students to public universities.

The Research University
and Its Responsibilities

The Numbers Game and
Graduate Education

October 1996

The National Science Board report *Science and Engineering Indicators, 1996* has a new section this year, entitled "Science and Engineering Labor Market."[1] It begins with the following statement: "The performance of the U.S. economy is the major determinant of current and future demand for scientists and engineers." I would argue that this statement represents a short-term perspective on the science and engineering labor market. Clearly, the current economy determines the flow of taxes, company revenues, and the number of individuals who will be hired at any given time. A long-term perspective, however, would focus on the importance of science and engineering as a driver of the future economy; the investments made in R&D today will be a dominating factor in the level of economic growth experienced in the future.

In your packet for this conference on graduate education in the biological sciences, you have an article on the supply and demand for scientists and engineers that I published in *Science* in 1990, based on work done in 1988.[2] This article reported on a National Science Foundation study that I was involved in, much like the study that Bill Bowen and a colleague at Princeton were doing at about the same time.[3] Bill and I were both projecting a significant future shortfall of Ph.D.'s. Bowen was looking at the humanities and the social sciences as well as the natural sciences and engineering. My paper was concerned only with the natural sciences and engineering and excluded the social sciences. The study began with the year 1988 and projected the supply of Ph.D.'s that would be trained in future years. That projection was made on the assumption that a certain percent of undergraduate students would go on for Ph.D.'s, and thus was based on the demographics of the twenty-two-year-old population. If you look back over the past twenty years, the proportion of twenty-two-year-olds who eventually earned a Ph.D. in science and engineering is remarkably stable.

Added to that was the assumption that the number of foreign students taking Ph.D.'s in the United States in future years would remain at the 1988 level. In 1988 we had a large number of foreign students taking Ph.D.'s, and the assumption was that this number wouldn't increase significantly. A further assumption was that 50 percent of the foreign students who earned Ph.D.'s in the United States would stay in the United States. And these assumptions led to the wiggly curve on the chart labeled "Supply of Ph.D.'s." You can see on the far left [of the chart] the actual number of Ph.D.'s produced in 1988. Supply was projected through the year 2010.

The D_0 curve was based on the assumption that the future demand for Ph.D.'s would remain constant. That is, whatever

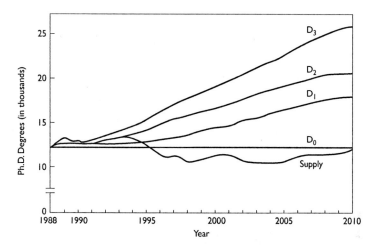

Supply and demand projected to the year 2010 for Ph.D.'s in the natural sciences and engineering. Four demand scenarios are indicated by the D_0, D_1, D_2, and D_3 curves.

the demand was in 1988, that demand would stay the same out to the year 2010. Note that for the D_0 demand curve, it is not until the late 1990s that an undersupply of Ph.D.'s begins to occur.

But the constant D_0 scenario seemed highly unlikely for at least three reasons. First, yearly replacements due to retirements and deaths were expected to increase over the next two decades. Second, we considered it almost certain that college and university enrollments would increase in the late 1990s with the expanding college-age population, necessitating an increase in the number of faculty hired. Third, we assumed that if federal and private investments in R&D continued to grow at even moderate rates, the number of new Ph.D.'s required by industry would be well above the 1988 level. These three factors generate four cumulative demand scenarios, labeled D_0, D_1, D_2, and D_3.

We knew the demographics of the workforce in 1988 and the age distribution of Ph.D.'s in that workforce, and therefore it was fairly easy to predict the expected increase in the number of retirements. If one assumed that for every Ph.D. who retired, a replacement would enter the workforce, the result is the D_1 curve. If you compare the D_1 curve with the supply curve, somewhere after the year 2000 you begin to see a significant divergence; an increase in Ph.D. production would have to occur in order to have an adequate supply.

Another factor was the number of undergraduates enrolled in universities. We could predict with assurance that there would be a significant increase in the number of college-age students by the late '90s. If one assumed that the ratio of faculty to students would be maintained at the 1988 level, then one would add to the D_1 curve and predict a demand for Ph.D.'s represented by the D_2 curve. Finally, assuming there would be growth in the number of Ph.D.'s required in the nonacademic workforce, it seemed sensible to add a growth factor of 4 percent, which cumulated to the D_3 curve. After all, the private sector workforce was expected to expand, and one would expect a correlated increase in the need for Ph.D.'s.[4] These four demand curves represented projections based on a well-defined set of assumptions. And depending on which curve you believed, you could get quite exercised about the projected shortfall. Once I published the 1990 paper, and once Bill Bowen published his work, considerable unhappiness ensued in the academic world as the job market began to deteriorate. The fact is, however, that both sets of projections did not identify significant shortfalls in the supply of Ph.D.'s until the late '90s.

What has happened since the publication of the 1990 *Science* paper? One unanticipated factor was the end of the cold war, with the resulting cutbacks in defense spending. Another factor was that the number of foreign students taking Ph.D.'s in the United States did not remain constant, as we assumed, but instead has grown at a significant rate. And in 1988 I thought a greater proportion of foreign students would choose to return to their country of origin than had been the case in the past, because those countries were becoming more competitive and more attractive for young Ph.D.'s. It turns out that the proportion that remained in the United States did not decline, but rather increased.

What else has changed? Colleges and universities across the nation haven't yet experienced the kind of increase in enrollments that will be coming. Further, the student-faculty ratio has not remained constant, but rather has deteriorated. For example, at the University of California, it has changed from a ratio of about 14:1 up to almost 19:1. I hope the student-faculty ratio will return to more favorable levels in the future, but for the moment it is a clear indicator that the nation is investing fewer resources in educating college students.

Another factor was the Immigration Act of 1990. This act specified categories of individuals seeking to immigrate who had particular skills and gave them added consideration. As a result of this legislation, a large number of foreign-trained Ph.D.'s have entered the U.S. labor force. Twenty-three percent of the Ph.D.'s employed in the United States today were born in another country.[5] We now have the highest percent in history of foreign-born Ph.D.'s in the United States workforce.

So the question is: Is there an oversupply of Ph.D.'s? Several weeks ago I read in the *New York Times Magazine* an article by a professor of history about the serious employment problems facing Ph.D.'s, particularly in the humanities, where the placement rate for new Ph.D.'s in history and English, for example, is less than 50 percent.[6] It was a wrenching article. Without question, there are disturbing problems in the humanities. Are there problems in science and engineering? That depends on whom you talk to. In physics, there is no doubt that we have a problem. But consider a field like engineering. If you're a Ph.D. electrical engineer or a computer scientist, there is an oversupply of jobs. In mechanical engineering, on the other hand, there is a shortage of jobs.

In recent years, the Science Indicators Report has included a new measure designated "involuntary/outside of field," meaning Ph.D.'s who cannot find appropriate work and have been forced to work outside of their area of expertise. The fields of geophysics, physics, and mechanical engineering are the three highest in terms of the percent of individuals who fall into the involuntary/outside of field category. The figure is 7.7 percent for geophysics and about 6.5 percent each for astronomy, physics, and mechanical engineering. (For a few other fields: biological science, 2.1 percent; computer science, 1.4 percent; and chemistry, 3.5 percent.)

The point is that Ph.D. employment is very much a field-by-field issue. A close friend of mine took a Ph.D. in astronomy—a first-rate degree and a first-rate talent. He now runs a software company. You can imagine his history: As an astronomer he did a great deal of work on instrumentation, which involved sophisticated computer programming. He tried for many years to land a regular faculty position, but eventually gave up. He then started his own software company and has done spectacularly well. Is he inappropriately matched to his Ph.D. program? Was it a mistake for the United States to invest in his training in astronomy? I think not. And the biotech business would not be thriving in California if we did not have a steady flow of Ph.D.'s from our universities.

Despite problems in a number of fields, therefore, it is disturbing to hear some people make the blanket statement that we are training too many Ph.D.'s. Certainly physicists and scholars in the humanities will resonate with that notion. But to jump to the conclusion that the nation faces an across-the-board oversupply of scientists and engineers is inaccurate and misleading.

This doesn't mean we can't improve the preparation of Ph.D. students. I'm enthusiastic about the National Research Council's recommendation to reduce time to degree. I also support the idea that the training of Ph.D.'s should be more versatile so that they have greater opportunities in the job market. And the council's recommendation for a national employment database for science and engineering Ph.D.'s should be an immediate priority. Such a database would be invaluable to faculty advisors and to students as they plan their future. Further, if it were accessible on the Internet, we would quickly realize that the information we're collecting is inadequate. We'd begin to expand and refine our database and have more relevant information. So I support the council's recommendations, particularly as a way to match more closely societal needs with the training of Ph.D.'s in various subfields of science and engineering.

The University of California is a major player in graduate education. We produce about 10 percent of the nation's Ph.D.'s. Until this year, we have had a formula-driven budgeting process for graduate enrollments that makes little sense in the current environment. To greatly simplify, from about 1960 until this year, the number of doctoral students in a given discipline was principally determined by the number of undergraduates in that discipline. A large number of psychology undergraduates translated into a large number of psychology graduate students. The formula wasn't quite that simpleminded—and did take account of field-to-field differences—but that was the basic idea. With much discussion among the faculty and little public fanfare, we've changed our budgeting process. The change takes effect this year. No longer will we tie the number of graduate students to undergraduate enrollment, field by field. We now have a budget process in which departments will not lose budgetary support if they cut back in their graduate enrollments. Until last year, departments had to have large numbers of graduate students in order to receive the full set of rewards that the system had to offer. We are now changing our budgetary system so that the number of Ph.D. students in a department is driven more heavily by the job market and employment opportunities.

Let me conclude by saying that the training of Ph.D.'s to meet the nation's needs is one of the most important questions facing higher education, now and into the twenty-first century. We must be very careful about how we think about graduate education and the marketplace—taking into account both short-term and long-term perspectives. We would do ourselves and the nation a disservice if we came to a blanket generalization that our research universities are producing too many Ph.D.'s. The problem is too complex and too important to the nation's future to yield to simpleminded solutions.

NOTES

This paper was presented at the Conference on Graduate Education in the Biological Sciences in the Twenty-first Century, San Francisco, October 2, 1996.

1. National Science Board, *Science and Engineering Indicators, 1996* (Washington, D.C.: U.S. Government Printing Office, 1996).

2. Richard C. Atkinson, "Supply and Demand for Scientists and Engineers: A National Crisis in the Making," *Science* 248 (April 27, 1990).

3. W. G. Bowen and J. A. Sosa, *Prospects for Faculty in the Arts and Sciences* (Princeton, N.J.: Princeton University Press, 1989).

4. To save time, I have provided a very cursory explanation of these projections. My original article in *Science* should be consulted for a more detailed account.

5. National Science Board, *Science and Engineering Indicators, 1996.*

6. Louis Menand, "How to Make a Ph.D. Matter," *New York Times Magazine,* September 22, 1996.

Opportunities for Chinese and American Universities in the Knowledge-Based Economy

October 1999

It is a great pleasure to be back in China. I first came here in 1978 as director of the National Science Foundation [NSF] to explore the possibility of an exchange of students, scholars, and scientists between our two countries. The Chinese government had expressed an interest in such an exchange; the White House was taken by surprise but quickly agreed to talks, with one proviso—that such an exchange would require a formal "memorandum of understanding" signed by the two governments. What has been called the Nixon-Kissinger ping-pong diplomacy occurred earlier, but it had not led to a normalization of relations. The Chinese initially insisted on an informal arrangement for an exchange but eventually agreed to a government-to-government program. I wish I had time today to give you an account of our negotiations. Suffice it to say that each side had a great deal to learn from the other. I signed the exchange memorandum for the United States; it was the first document ever cosigned by the two governments. Soon thereafter, our exchange program became part of a more comprehensive agreement on science and technology that Chairman Deng and President Carter signed on the chairman's historic visit to the United States in January 1979.

Today, as we celebrate the twentieth anniversary of that agreement, it is gratifying to see the growing interest that scientists and government officials in China have shown in the contributions of basic research to their country's overall development. This science policy seminar is a fitting tribute to the crucial role that scientific ties established two decades ago have come to play in the relationship between our two nations.

I believe that building a strong foundation of basic research will ensure China's future economic competitiveness. This approach has been used with success in the United States for over fifty years. How this focus on basic research evolved, and the role that research universities play in spurring American economic growth, are the principal themes of this lecture. I will conclude with some thoughts about the challenges Chinese universities face in today's knowledge-based economy.

The term *knowledge-based economy*—sometimes called the "new economy"—refers to a set of industries whose main products or services use information to decrease costs and create new opportunities for growth. Generally speaking, the industries of the new economy tend to produce jobs more rapidly and with higher salaries, increase productivity growth faster, and provide greater profits for employers than the "old" economy. These high-technology industries rely on a constant infusion of new knowledge to stay competitive, and the principal source of such knowledge is basic research. The California economy provides a striking example. Its recovery from the economic recession of the early 1990s depended on knowledge-driven businesses and jobs that didn't exist fifteen or twenty years ago—biotechnology, telecommunications, and multimedia, for example.

The evidence regarding the relationship between research and development (R&D) and economic growth in the United States is overwhelming. As recently as the early 1970s, there was no substantial economic analysis of the relationship between investments in R&D and economic development. When I served as director of the National Science Foundation in the 1970s, we were well aware of the lack of such economic data in making the case to the Congress for federal support of research. And we realized that most of our arguments about how R&D affected economic growth were based on little more than anecdotal evidence. Accordingly, we initiated a special research program at NSF focused on just that issue—the relationship between investments in R&D and the growth of the American economy.

In the intervening twenty-five years, a substantial body of research has led to a development in economics called "new growth theory." The influence of this work can be seen in a 1995 report of President Clinton's Council of Economic Advisers, which notes that 50 percent of the growth in the American economy in the last forty years has been due to investments in research and development. The private sector is a major source of R&D, but federally funded research at universities also plays a key role. The report points out that when federal investments in university research increase, there is—with an appropriate time lag—a corresponding increase in private-sector investments.

There is now a well-understood link between university-based research and industries' R&D efforts.

As I mentioned, the State of California provides one of the best examples of this linkage. In the early 1990s, the state endured one of the worst economic recessions in its history. California in prior periods had entered economic recessions later, and come out much earlier, than the rest of the United States. But in the 1990s this traditional pattern broke down. California suffered a brutal economic downturn fueled by tremendous cutbacks in defense and aerospace—a loss of jobs that resulted in a dramatic drop in the tax revenues of the state.

What has happened in the past few years? California has come storming back from the recession. Why? New jobs have been created at a fast rate. Where are those jobs coming from? From a particular type of activity: high technology. And these high-tech enterprises are not the vast IBMs and AT&Ts of the world. The companies that pulled California out of recession are small, entrepreneurial high-tech ventures. These companies (and their technologies) can be traced directly to the research universities of California, both public and private.

Biotechnology, for example, a booming industry in California, traces its success—in fact its very existence—to research programs that came out of the state's universities. Digital telecommunications is another case in point. It could not exist at its current scale and scope without the California universities that produce the research and educate the engineers and scientists essential to keeping this industry on the cutting edge.

California succeeded in its remarkable economic comeback because it possessed four advantages essential to the new economy: (1) world-class research universities that encourage faculty—and allow them to benefit financially—when they are involved in research that leads to the development of new technologies; (2) a supply of entrepreneurs experienced in launching and developing high-technology businesses; (3) venture capital and other sources of private investment in early-stage business ventures; and (4) the accounting, legal, and other ancillary services needed by start-up companies.

I would like to mention a concrete example, one that I am familiar with because it began while I was chancellor of the San Diego campus of the University of California (UCSD). In the early 1980s, the San Diego region was in the midst of a painful economic transition created by the demise of many of its defense-related industries. It was clear that something was needed to bridge the gap, but what? My colleagues and I decided that UCSD had to play a more aggressive role in regional economic growth, specifically in the high-technology and biotechnology areas. Our view was that small high-technology corporations were the most likely candidates to fill the economic vacuum that followed reductions in defense contracts to many San Diego corporations. UCSD had specific strengths it could contribute to the high-technology sector: the campus is one of the nation's top recipients of federal research funding; it is home to strong science departments and an excellent school of engineering.

We expanded the breadth of UCSD's basic research capacity, creating—in cooperation with industry—interdisciplinary research centers in such areas as magnetic recording, molecular genetics, wireless communications, and structural engineering. We reinvigorated our technology-transfer programs in the science and engineering departments. And we created a program called UCSD CONNECT, which had as its goal not only technology transfer but also nurturing the business support in-frastructure that has proven essential to small entrepreneurial firms. UCSD CONNECT draws on expertise across all cam-pus departments and from all professional sectors. It has served to fill a critical gap in San Diego's business infrastructure, link-ing local high-tech entrepreneurs with financial, managerial, and technical resources.

What this means, for example, is that UCSD CONNECT will act as an agent on behalf of small companies to help them locate investors and find the research they need to develop new products. Working with start-up companies as early as the busi-ness-plan stage, UCSD CONNECT will help an entrepreneur find contacts for raising capital, form strategic alliances, and gain marketing and management expertise and technical ad-vice. UCSD CONNECT is often referred to as an "incubator without walls," because it has nurtured so many successful busi-nesses in San Diego.

UCSD CONNECT is just one model of the kind of help U.C. is committed to providing. There are similar efforts on every one of U.C.'s campuses to bring venture capitalists and people from the industrial sector together with U.C. scientists and engineers to move research ideas into application.

A recent example is the Industry-University Cooperative Re-search Program [IUCRP], a University-wide effort now in its fourth year, which seeks to identify the most promising research areas for new products. A U.C. researcher joins with a scien-tist or engineer from a private company to formulate a research proposal. A panel of experts drawn from industry and academia then selects the best proposals for funding. Industry investments are partially matched with University funds.

An important feature of the program is the opportunity for graduate students to participate in research. It would be difficult to overstate the crucial link between research and graduate education in American universities. Graduate students participate in all aspects of faculty research projects. This experience is an essential part of the educational process for graduate students; it produces both excellent young faculty for universities and R&D leaders for industry. In the case of the IUCRP, graduate students learn first-hand about industry's needs and its opportunities. And industry gets the benefit of some of the world's brightest young minds.

Two-thirds of the 323 companies currently participating in the IUCRP are small businesses. A particularly valuable benefit for them is the opportunity to work with U.C. faculty on multidisciplinary research that would be difficult or impossible to pursue in the private sector. Research supported by the IUCRP lays the foundation for next-generation technologies. The six industrial sectors that currently participate—biotechnology, communications, information technology, microelectronics, multimedia, and semiconductor manufacturing—are all critical to the California economy.

There is growing interest in programs like these not only in California but throughout the United States. The impetus for greater linkages between universities and industry grows out of a longstanding American belief that universities should not be divorced from society, but should be involved in helping solve society's problems.

The United States is unusual in the degree to which it relies on universities to perform basic research. The roots of this phenomenon date back over fifty years to World War II. Near the end of the war, President Roosevelt turned to his science advisor, Vannevar Bush, for advice about the future of American science. Bush's report, which appeared shortly after President Roosevelt's death, was entitled *Science: The Endless Frontier*. As the title suggests, Bush viewed science as a vast frontier of opportunities to serve virtually every aspect of the national welfare. His report set the stage for the modern era of science and technology in the United States.

What were the arguments that Vannevar Bush put forward? First of all, he asked, "Who should fund the research and development effort of the United States?" Let me make a few distinctions here.

For simplicity of expression, I will use the terms *basic research, applied research,* and *development*. Basic research is not focused on applications; the terms *curiosity research* and *discovery research* are sometimes used to describe it. It is driven by a sheer interest in the phenomena rather than potential applications. But basic research may reach a stage where there is potential for application and, accordingly, a need for applied research and, in turn, the development of new products and processes. Bush argued that applied research and development should be done by the private sector, by industry. But he also argued that the private sector would not provide adequate funding for basic research. In essence, he believed that private-market mechanisms ensured that industry would invest in applied research and development, but that those same private-market mechanisms would not generate adequate investment in basic research. Thus, he concluded that the funding of basic research was an obligation of the federal government.

The second question he asked was, "Who should perform R&D activities?" Applied research and development, he said, is a private-sector responsibility; the private sector could be relied upon to perform that kind of activity. Who should perform basic research? The Bush concept, founded on the experiences of World War II, was that American universities should be the principal performers of basic research; and, as noted above, the federal government should provide the funds for that work.

Then there was a third part to Bush's analysis. He believed that basic research should be funded through a peer-review process. Individual scientists should make proposals for research projects, and a group of peers—leading scientists from around the country—should evaluate these proposals and decide which to fund and which not to fund.

Federal science agencies in the United States do not provide unrestricted block-grant funding to universities. Rather, individual scientists submit proposals that request funding for specific research projects. A scientist's proposal is then sent to other scientists for their evaluation and judged competitively against other research efforts. This evaluation—the peer-review process—is the critical factor in ensuring that the best science is funded.

Those were Bush's arguments: applied research and development should be funded and conducted by the private sector; basic research should be performed in universities and be funded by the federal government via a peer-review process. The Bush model created a sea change for American universities. Before World War II, universities were peripheral to the R&D enterprise. Today, they are at the center of American research activities, thanks in large measure to an extraordinarily successful partnership with the federal government. As a result, both the research enterprise itself and the U.S. economy have prospered. I do not believe it is an overstatement to say that when the history of the last half of the twentieth century is written, the role research universities have played in the American economy will be regarded as one of our greatest accomplishments.

In recent years, there has been much discussion in the United States about the need for a new national science policy, on the premise that Bush's fifty-year-old vision cannot provide a blueprint for the twenty-first century. It is true that some of the arguments in Bush's report are now questionable; some of the issues he considered important are of interest only to students of the period. What remains pertinent is his vision of the role of government in research, including his assertion that the federal government has both the authority and the obligation to support basic research. More boldly, by arguing for the primacy of basic research supported according to norms set by scientists themselves, Bush implicitly asserted that universities defined the U.S. research enterprise. Bush gave them pride of place at the center because, as he argued, they had the potential to energize the entire system.

In spite of these remarkable successes, there is a concern in the United States today that federal funding for basic research will decline as the government struggles to balance its budget. The president of the United States and the Congress have reaffirmed their commitment to keeping the federal budget balanced and to using a part of the surplus to reduce the national debt. Although some of the predictions about draconian cuts in federal funding for research have not so far materialized, this remains a matter of concern to universities throughout the nation.

The potential erosion of federal support for academic research is worrisome precisely because of the central role universities play in the overall R&D effort. Could industry take their place as the vital center of the American research enterprise? The evidence suggests not. As recently as a decade ago, several large U.S. firms performed significant basic research in their corporate laboratories. Today, virtually all industrial research focuses on the solution of specific problems, often by building on the results of university research. AT&T and IBM have essentially pulled out of basic research; both companies have come to the view that they are not wealthy enough to support basic research—at least not at the level they once did. In the United States we are relying more than ever on universities for the basic research that will ultimately fuel our economy. A recent statistic sums it up: 73 percent of the papers cited by U.S. industry patents are based on publicly supported science, authored principally by university scientists; only 27 percent are authored by industrial scientists.

I am more optimistic than many of my colleagues that the federal government will find a way to continue funding university research at a reasonable level. Most political leaders in the United States who have thought about these issues—Democrats and Republicans alike—have concluded that support of our research enterprise is critical to the national interest, and therefore to sound federal policy.

In its simplicity and flexibility, Bush's report remains a model for science policy in the United States. But does Bush's model have any relevance for contemporary China and its universities?

Obviously, no model can be imported wholesale from one country into another. China is finding its own way and its own solutions to the challenge of putting knowledge to work in the economy. But however solutions differ, more and more nations are coming to the realization that their universities are priceless sources of ideas that can create jobs, give birth to new industries, and stimulate the productivity growth that will enable them to create a better life for their people.

Among China's advantages today are growing encouragement for private enterprise and entrepreneurship within the country, and increasing interest among foreign investors in China's strengths in such areas as software, materials science, and biotechnology. One example of this interest is Microsoft's and Intel's decision to establish research centers here. Most important of all are the incredible resources China possesses in its universities and in its talented young people. Many of these young people have studied at foreign institutions and have experiences that will be very valuable to them in today's international marketplace.

This point brings me back to where I began—to the importance of international exchange in educating new generations of scientists and engineers who can function effectively in other countries and other cultures. This science policy seminar will surely reveal new directions our countries need to take, but it is also a wonderful reminder of how far we have come from those tentative contacts of twenty years ago.

We are living in one of history's most productive eras of intellectual discovery. From agriculture to medicine, from aerospace to computing, science is experiencing a series of revolutions that are remaking our ideas of what is possible. These revolutions are occurring on the campuses and laboratories of research universities every day. We have only just begun to tap the possibilities of this explosion of knowledge, and the effort to link intellectual discovery more closely to applications has major implications for economies around the world. Universities are key to this effort.

Let me conclude by pointing out that in the United States, the nation's most distinguished research universities are members of an organization called the Association of American Universities. The AAU includes sixty-two universities—not a large number in comparison with the 3,700 institutions that make up the American higher education system. (It should be noted that six of the AAU institutions are campuses of the University of California.) But, for reasons I have explored in this paper, these sixty-two institutions have an impact on America's prospects far out of proportion to their numbers. In a world in which scientific knowledge doubles every twelve to fifteen years, research universities are clearly an important element in any nation's economic strategy. And as impressive as their past accomplishments have been, the possibilities are so plentiful, and the potential is so enormous, that the most exciting days for research universities lie not behind us but ahead.

NOTES

This paper was delivered at the China-U.S. Joint Science Policy Seminar, Beijing, People's Republic of China, October 25, 1999.

The Globalization of the University

May 2001

We are living in an age of unprecedented intellectual discovery, an era in which knowledge doubles every twelve to fifteen years in the sciences alone. Thanks to revolutionary advances in telecommunications, we are also living in an age of unprecedented dissemination of knowledge. Our rapidly expanding ability to share information and ideas is leading to what can be called the globalization of the university. By "globalization" I mean the forces that are transforming the university from an institution with a monopoly on knowledge to one among many different types of organizations serving as information providers, and from an institution that has always been circumscribed by time and geography to one without boundaries.

For universities, globalization means:

· Information and communication technologies—the Internet and the World Wide Web, streaming and interactive video—are providing powerful new tools to forge global networks for teaching and research. To date, most forms of online learning have relied on platforms that are too primitive for high-quality interactions. Dramatic educational breakthroughs will occur when the platform is versatile enough to support rich visual and auditory displays, reacts quickly to student inputs, can acquire and use information about an individual student's style of learning, and is reliable and easy to use. The prerequisite technology may not quite be here yet, but it will be soon, especially with the introduction of high-speed wireless platforms.

· In this new environment, one organization—whether it is a university or a private corporation—can serve the needs and reap the rewards of worldwide markets. The global university could teach students anywhere (and thanks to the Internet, at any time) and draw its faculty from around the world.

· Universities no longer have a monopoly on the production of knowledge. They will be competing with suppliers of information and ideas who have no need of expensive campuses, athletic fields, or faculty clubs. In a much-quoted interview a few years ago, American management expert Peter Drucker said that "thirty years from now the big university campus will be a relic. Universities won't survive in their present form. The main reason is the shift to the continuing education of already highly educated adults as the center and growth sector of education."

And indeed, competitors to the traditional freestanding university are springing up around the world. They range from for-profit ventures like the University of Phoenix and Fathom.com, to equity stakes in private companies (UNext.com, for example, enlists universities to provide course content), to licensing agreements of various kinds, to university consortia like Universitas 21, a group of eighteen European, North American, and Australian universities, or the Alliance for Lifelong Learning, organized by Stanford, Yale, Oxford, and Princeton universities. Investors poured billions of dollars into online learning last year, and projections are that it is a growth industry. The United Kingdom has announced its intention to establish an e-university, and the European Union plans to do the same.

The enormous international demand for technical and professional training will encourage new providers of higher education to cross boundaries and offer teaching anytime, anywhere. But we do not know whether a large enough global market will emerge for online education; whether most students will choose subjects that promise immediate financial or career benefits, as opposed to liberal arts curricula; or whether traditional higher education will dominate the market. This is an entirely new world for which there are no models.

For universities, the biggest challenge of globalization is to their institutional structures and habits of mind. I would like to briefly discuss three issues that globalization raises for universities: accreditation, intellectual property, and maintaining the university as a community.

ACCREDITATION

Technology may be making the university global in its reach, but some things about education remain stubbornly local. One of those things is accreditation. A major aspect of education is its role in credentialing students—those who pass the appropriate courses or examinations receive a degree. Educational institutions can credential students because they are licensed to do so by governmental or quasi-governmental agencies, whether national or local. But there are no global accrediting bodies, which is one reason critics of online learning view it as a threat to academic quality. Universitas 21, the consortium of universities I mentioned a moment ago, is betting that one of its degrees will have the same value in the academic marketplace as a traditional degree from, say, the University of California or the Nagasaki University of Foreign Studies.

But can an educational institution really accredit students anywhere in the world? For the kind of professional and corporate training that Peter Drucker mentions, perhaps the answer is yes. However, for traditional undergraduate and graduate education in the arts and sciences, the answer is far from certain. The University of California consists of ten campuses, and credits earned at one campus are not automatically transferable to another. If such a barrier exists between campuses within a single university system, what are the barriers likely to be between nations? When I was a faculty member at Stanford University in California, some of my graduate students were French. Many did years of graduate study at Stanford but returned to the University of Paris when the time came to write their doctoral dissertations, even though the work leading up to the dissertation had been done at Stanford. Why? Because submitting their thesis to a French university meant a French degree, and all the opportunities for advancement a doctoral degree from the "right" university bestows on an ambitious young French academic. A degree from a foreign university would not open the same doors or have the same value. Students have a finely honed instinct for such matters.

This is not just a question of rules and regulations but of reputation and confidence. People tend to have confidence in institutions they know, and most of those institutions are local. The value of state and local colleges and universities will remain despite the universality of the Web.

INTELLECTUAL PROPERTY

A second challenge globalization presents is also something of a paradox: while Web-based learning is creating new avenues to knowledge, it is generating new constraints as well. Universities, by long tradition, share knowledge freely and widely. But in a society in which they are no longer the dominant creators and disseminators of knowledge, the rules of the game change dramatically. Universities have less and less access to intellectual output as control of scholarly communication continues to be commercialized and concentrated among a few large companies like Reed-Elsevier, which is notorious for soaring journal prices and high profit margins. And individuals and institutions in the private sector that offer courses or conduct research expect to be paid for the use of their intellectual property—as do some universities that are beginning to market courses online.

This trend has been described as the "privatization of knowledge," and it is a challenge to the role that universities have played for centuries as places where information and ideas are open to anyone. Because we are a knowledge-based society, however, ideas and their applications bring new wealth that can be difficult to resist—wealth that hard-pressed universities can use for such worthy ends as increasing faculty salaries or otherwise supporting the academic enterprise.

But this is a controversial area for universities. Just last month, the Massachusetts Institute of Technology drew worldwide attention when it announced that, in "an effort to create a model for university dissemination of knowledge in the Internet age," it would make available to anyone on the Web the materials used in courses taught at MIT. This program, called OpenCourseWare, is expected to cost one hundred million dollars, which the university hopes to pay for through private gifts, and take ten years to complete. It is also voluntary; MIT faculty who do not wish to participate are not required to do so. OpenCourseWare is not unique in making course materials available on the Web—many faculty at the University of California and elsewhere do the same thing. But no other institution has done it on this scale, and planners at MIT regard the OpenCourseWare program as a statement about preserving the basic mission of the university in an increasingly commercialized academic environment. In this new world, intellectual property issues are taking on vast new importance.

THE UNIVERSITY AS COMMUNITY

There is another issue raised by globalization in addition to accreditation and intellectual property: the traditional organization of university life. Globalization challenges universities to overcome the ancient competitiveness of academic institutions. Universities in the United States and elsewhere have always competed with each other for faculty, students, resources, and prestige. Even within a university system, campuses compete with each other; faculty do not have tenure within the University of California system, but at a specific U.C. campus. Consortia like the Alliance for Lifelong Learning, whose members include Oxford, Yale, Princeton, and Stanford universities, try to bring together institutions that have long been rivals. The globalization of the university is giving birth to new forms of cooperation, but it is also generating more competition, not less. It is too soon to know whether the pressures for cooperation will turn out to be stronger than the habit of competition.

And it is far from certain that online learning will be welcomed enthusiastically by faculty in every discipline. One promising area for online learning is basic courses in subjects many students take, like composition or calculus. As online courses become more sophisticated, they may reach the point where faculty do not need to be involved at all. The faculty who teach these classes, however, are also the faculty who conduct the research necessary to future advances in the field. This reality applies to disciplines across the board: if basic classes in major disciplines were to migrate entirely online, there is reason for concern about what happens to faculty in research universities, who keep their disciplines and their institutions at the forefront of discovery.

Further, some faculty see online learning as a threat to quality, that fundamental value of academic life. If faculty are involved in online learning to the same extent they are in a real classroom—responding to questions, evaluating student performance, preparing course materials, advising on future courses a student might need—the cost to the university doesn't vary much from the cost of offering a class on campus. But if faculty are not deeply engaged in shaping students' course of study, how do we ensure that students get an excellent education?

The answer to these questions is: we don't know yet. One of the most fascinating imponderables involves the coming generations who will benefit from the new learning technologies. We do not know enough about the students of the future. Will these students, raised on the Web, want the same kind of education their parents did? When Stanford University began offering students the option of taking engineering classes online, many deserted the classroom entirely. We know that, at U.C., students frequently resort to the Web rather than to the campus library as a source of information. Given a choice, many will not choose an online video lecture as a substitute for attending classes, especially if the lecture is excellent. But students do use online lectures as study aids. Student choice—and perhaps student demand for more attention and service from their online professors—could be a powerful shaping force in future online learning.

WHAT WE KNOW

There are some things we do know. Scholarship and research are the foundation of the research university; education based on something other than those two activities is not in its tradition. This means that faculty, as the source of the central activities of the research university, must be deeply involved in forging the response of their institutions to the challenges of globalization.

We also know that, so far at least, no other organization has emerged that rivals the research university in the two vital activities of scholarship and research, or capitalizes as well on the way research and teaching nourish each other. And so far no other organization offers the array of services universities encompass, from the residential undergraduate experience to cultural events for the community to (in America at least) football for the alumni. Research universities are also where some of the most exciting experiments in online learning are taking place.

Because I have highlighted some of the problematic dimensions of globalization in these remarks, you may think that I am less than enthusiastic about the revolution in learning brought on by the new technologies. Nothing could be further from the truth.

For one thing, the new technologies are going to make it easier for students and faculty from different cultures and countries to work together. In March, the University of California and a number of Mexican universities celebrated the completion of a high-speed link, known as Internet2, between California and Mexico. Internet2 will make possible revolutionary Web applications that support collaborative teaching, research, and other cooperative ventures between the University of California and Mexican universities.

Here in Japan, U.C. is involved in a first-of-its-kind experiment in international academic cooperation called TIDE—that stands for Trans-Pacific Interactive Distance Education. In the fall of 1999, Kyoto University and U.C.'s Los Angeles campus (UCLA) began offering a course in physics taught simultaneously on both sides of the Pacific. Lectures delivered at one university are transmitted to the other through a high-speed link. Students at both locations can ask questions—and receive immediate answers—from the professors and get involved in discussions with other students. Lectures, assignments, demonstrations, and class interactions are archived so that both students and instructors can access them whenever they want. The program has been expanded to include introductory physics, communications studies, applied linguistics, and economics. It is a valuable lesson not only in technologically mediated instruction, but also in how students from different cultures interact in a classroom setting and how to create a collaborative learning environment.

Still another example will be of particular interest to you because it involves language acquisition. University of California faculty are launching a project that will use computers, multimedia, and interactive Web sites to teach the Spanish language. Called "Spanish without Walls," it will be a completely virtual course, taught entirely outside the classroom. CD-ROMs will allow students to take an interactive tour of all twenty-one Spanish-speaking countries, hear the dialects of different regions, and see videos on each country's culture and geography. Plans are to test the effectiveness of the course in spring 2002 by comparing the language proficiency of students who participate in Spanish without Walls this fall with that of students who take Spanish in a traditional classroom setting.

The new technologies are presenting other intriguing opportunities. One is the chance for controlled experiments on optimizing the learning process. We can create an online course with several variations, in which some students take one variant and other students take another. As students progress through the different variations of the course, we can collect data online that will enable us to test different hypotheses about the nature of the learning process. What we will have, in effect, is an educational laboratory that can answer important pedagogical questions: What is the optimal order in which to present ideas to make them easier to grasp? As a course unfolds, it should not unfold the same way for everyone. How can we tailor courses to the idiosyncratic abilities, motivations, preferences, and proclivities of each student? It is possible to devise course programs that maintain an online history of the student's performance and, based on that history, present course material in a way that is best for that particular student's learning style. The potential for truly individualized instruction is enormous.

For all its revolutionary possibilities, online learning is not going to spell the end of the university. Peter Drucker is wrong. Just as television and satellite TV have not replaced the live theater—which has a history going back millennia—so the new forms of learning are not going to displace the old. Rather, they will continue to develop in parallel, each with its own distinctive advantages and limitations. Most online courses, for example, cannot be mounted on a shoestring; like movies, they can reach many people, but they also involve a great deal of technical talent and very high production costs. Not every course is worth the expense; some courses are more appropriately done in the time-honored fashion, just as some plays are more compelling when they are performed in a small theater rather than on a big screen. Ultimately, there will be a balance between Web-based and traditional efforts. Research universities are not going to be swept away in a technological revolution. They will change and adjust in an incremental way. So those who worry about the future of the university, in my view, would be better off worrying about something else, like how universities are going to pay for the technological infrastructure online learning demands. (The state of Missouri has found an entrepreneurial answer for its elementary and high schools: it has levied a tax on movie rentals to fund information technology.) One thing is clear: globalization is challenging universities to rethink their organization and responsibilities so that they can respond creatively to the new world they have helped to bring about. Among the possibilities globalization offers to individuals and institutions is the opportunity to contribute to the common good.

CALIFORNIA DIGITAL LIBRARY AND ESCHOLARSHIP

So far I have talked mostly about the contributions of the new technologies to teaching. Let me conclude with examples taken from the areas of research and scholarly communication. These examples are just a few of the many things going on at the University of California and its affiliated laboratories.

With the help of technology, the University of California has created the California Digital Library (CDL), a collaborative library in which our ten campuses share a knowledge commons. A major strategy for taking advantage of technology, the CDL was founded with the belief that knowledge resources should not be constrained by the size and location of an institution. U.C. does not need ten separate digital libraries. The CDL is a framework through which the University is leveraging its collective investments in scholarly content, in technology, and in human resources to meet challenges of the digital age and to address the burgeoning quantity of scholarly publication. Its primary goal is to seek innovative and cost-effective means to achieving comprehensive access to scholarly and scientific communication for all members of the University community.

Although the CDL has been successful at expanding access to digital publications, we recognize that the only way to achieve this goal of comprehensive access will be for institutions to play a much more active role in the dissemination of knowledge. Over the next decade, a significant challenge for research universities is to influence and develop sustainable models for managing scholarly information, including its production. Although the current mechanisms and relationships among authors, institutions, and publishers are firmly entrenched, I believe that technology makes this an auspicious time for universities to catalyze change, and have thus committed U.C. to playing a leadership role in supporting that change. Universities contribute to the shared pool of knowledge and depend on it for research and teaching, but engagement in these complementary activities is not generally linked. At U.C., we are bringing these activities together through CDL's eScholarship program.

The University's eScholarship initiative is a vehicle through which we are supporting faculty in their desires to innovate in scholarly communication; eScholarship provides a technical and organizational infrastructure to support dissemination of knowledge as well as to ensure long-term preservation and access. It is an experimental effort to test the capacities and costs of Internet-based publication models. Working with discipline-based communities over the past year, eScholarship has opened three digital repositories, has supported two new, digital, peer-reviewed journals, is collaborating with the University's press to create entirely new kinds of monographs that are linked to rich primary resources, and has begun to explore collaborations with scientific societies. We will learn from these experiments, and we need to be joined by others for universities to play more than a passive role in acquiring the knowledge upon which our research and teaching depend.

Finally, a story about how the new technologies are helping us identify and develop talent. The *New York Times* recently carried a story about a young Czech physics student who posted a paper on an electronic archive run by the Los Alamos National

Laboratory, a nuclear research laboratory managed by U.C. for the United States Department of Energy. The paper concerned an area of physics known as string theory, a topic few faculty in his university knew much about. The Los Alamos archive attracts two million visits a week, and as a result the paper came to the attention of some of the world's leading physicists in string theory. They found the undergraduate's work so impressive that efforts on his behalf eventually led to a scholarship to do doctoral study at an American university.

As this incident dramatically illustrates, technology is erasing boundaries and creating an international community of learning—"a new realm of research," in the words of the *New York Times* story. The Los Alamos archive enables scientists virtually anywhere in the world, however isolated or lacking in access to scientific equipment, to gain access to the cutting edge of discovery. Just as important, through the archive they can become involved in an international dialogue about the latest developments in their field. These outcomes would have been impossible even fifteen years ago.

Together, global connectivity and university leadership can create new patterns and new roles in teaching, scholarship, and research, and access to all three. It is up to us—and especially the faculty, who are the heart of the academic enterprise—to ensure that the new learning technologies serve the important goals for which universities were created centuries ago.

NOTES

These remarks were delivered at the inauguration of President Akimasa Mitsuta, Nagasaki University of Foreign Studies, Japan, May 26, 2001.

Academic Freedom and the
Research University

June 2003

When we imagine creating the modern research university de novo, the first cornerstone to be laid is that of academic freedom. The American idea of academic freedom originated in Europe; it was faculty trained in European universities who brought with them the concept to American universities. About half of the members of the 1915 American Association of University Professors (AAUP) committee that first articulated a statement of academic freedom in the United States were graduates of German universities.

Academic freedom was critical in enabling faculty first to free themselves from sectarian religious domination and later to resist secular political control. The modern research university could not have emerged absent this commitment to academic freedom. However, I believe that the principles upon which academic freedom is founded must be elaborated and modified in ways that are relevant to the responsibilities and circumstances of today's universities.

Earlier this year I proposed that the University of California adopt a new statement on academic freedom, a policy that was approved by the Assembly of the Academic Senate by a vote of 45 to 3. This new policy is both traditional and innovative. It respects tradition in that it affirms the three components of academic freedom—freedom of inquiry and research, freedom of teaching, and freedom of expression and publication. It breaks new ground in that it explicitly recognizes the means of maintaining those freedoms. The policy embraces the concept of the faculty as members of a profession with distinctive competencies and responsibilities; this concept is essential for the University to carry out its fundamental mission and essential to our policy on academic freedom.

COURSE ON PALESTINIAN POETICS

The new policy emerged from debates sparked by a heated controversy over a course on Palestinian literature. In spring 2003, a graduate student instructor at the Berkeley campus posted a description of his freshman composition course on the English department's Web site. The title of his course was "The Politics and Poetics of Palestinian Resistance." The course description explained that students would examine how Palestinians created literature "under the brutal weight of the Israeli occupation." The instructor's description made it clear that he was a staunch supporter of the Palestinians. His course description ended with the suggestion that "conservative thinkers are encouraged to seek other sections" of the course.

On its face, the instructor's course description was outrageous. It raised several immediate concerns: departmental oversight of the course; senior faculty supervision of graduate student instructors; the bases on which an instructor may limit enrollment; student rights and how they are protected. Berkeley chancellor Robert M. Berdahl, working closely with the Academic Senate, resolved these questions quickly and skillfully. Senior faculty spoke with the instructor to ensure that he understood his obligations and responsibilities as an instructor at the University. The course description was changed. Students taking the course were advised that they had the right to express themselves and have their work evaluated without discrimination or harassment. They were also informed that they could bring concerns to the chair of the English department. A senior faculty member sat in on all class meetings to ensure that the course was taught consistently with academic norms. In the end, the students who took the class gave outstanding ratings to both the course content and the instructor. (For a full account of the issues the course raised and how they were addressed, see the May–June 2003 issue of *Academe,* the bulletin of the American Association of University Professors.)

SPROUL STATEMENT ON ACADEMIC FREEDOM

The incident, however, revealed a fundamental weakness in the University's policies. When my colleague, Patrick Hayashi, and I examined U.C.'s academic freedom policy, we found that President Robert Gordon Sproul had first articulated it in 1934; it was formally adopted as University policy in 1944. The policy is published in the Academic Personnel Manual and referred to as "APM 010—Academic Freedom."

APM 010—Academic Freedom

The following announcement was originally made by the President of the University before the Northern Section of the Academic Senate on August 27, 1934, and is to be regarded as setting forth the principles which guide the President in these matters and accordingly stand as, in a certain sense, the policy of the University.

The function of the university is to seek and transmit knowledge and to train students in the processes whereby truth is to be made known. To convert, or make converts, is alien and hostile to this dispassionate duty. Where it becomes necessary, in performing this function of a university, to consider political, social or sectarian movements, they are dissected and examined—not taught, and the conclusion left, with no tipping of the scales, to the logic of the facts.

The University is founded upon faith in intelligence and knowledge and it must defend their free operation. It must rely upon truth to combat error. Its obligation is to see that the conditions upon which questions are examined are those which give play to intellect rather than to passion. Essentially the freedom of a university is the freedom of competent persons in the classroom. In order to protect this freedom, the University assumes the right to prevent exploitation of its prestige by unqualified persons or by those who would use it as a platform for propaganda. It therefore takes great care in the appointment of its teachers; it must take corresponding care with respect to others who wish to speak in its name.

The University respects personal belief as the private concern of the individual. It equally respects the constitutional rights of the citizen. It insists only that its members, as individuals and as citizens, shall likewise always respect—and not exploit—their University connections.

The University of California is a creature of the State and its loyalty to the State will never waver. It will not aid nor will it condone actions contrary to the laws of the State. Its high function—and its high privilege—the University will steadily continue to fulfill, serving the people by providing facilities for investigation and teaching free from domination by parties, sects, or selfish interests. The University expects the State, in return, to its own great gain, to protect this indispensable freedom, a freedom like the freedom of the press, that is the heritage and the right of a free people.

When President Sproul made this statement, California and the University were in turmoil. America was struggling with the Great Depression. There was tremendous labor unrest, often leading to large-scale demonstrations and strikes that ended in violence. A "Red scare" over a possible Communist takeover of the nation alarmed citizens and public officials alike. At that time, the traditional view of collegiate life reflected a belief that students, faculty, and administration were all part of a collegial family. However, some professors and students had a different view. They openly questioned the nature and purpose of American universities, arguing that, far from being the agents of advancement and democracy, they assisted in maintaining an oppressive status quo.

University of California faculty and students spoke out against the many problems facing the nation—poverty, corporate greed, racism, imperialism, and militarism. This activism offended powerful state politicians and civic leaders and, consequently, threatened the University's political and budgetary support. That was the context in which President Sproul issued his directive on academic freedom. Faculty would limit themselves to the "dispassionate" task of dissecting "the logic of the facts." In return, the state would "protect" the "indispensable freedom" of the University to "transmit knowledge." Political neutrality was the quid pro quo for political support—a bargain that enabled President Sproul to navigate the turbulent political waters of his time.

But the Sproul policy is not simply a relic of another generation's political wars. It also contains statements about academic freedom that few would disagree with, for example, the condemnation of using the classroom to make converts to a particular political view or to use the University as "a platform for propaganda." Yet when we looked to it for guidance on resolving the conflict over the Palestinian poetry class, the Sproul statement was unsatisfactory in important respects. Neutrality, the principle that undergirds the Sproul policy, does not constitute a sufficient criterion on which to decide cases of academic freedom. The logic of the facts can and does lead different people to dramatically different conclusions. Who decides what is partisan and what is not? Without criteria to make such distinctions, judgment must be made on other grounds. History has shown that those judgments are often based on whether or not the content of a faculty member's writings or remarks offends specific groups.

Furthermore, there is no necessary correlation between effective scholarship and neutrality, however the concept of neutrality may be defined. Faculty frequently hold strong viewpoints, many of which challenge prevailing orthodoxies. They routinely contribute to public discourse on a wide range of politically controversial subjects ranging from environmental hazards, welfare economics, and abortion policies to human cloning, religious doctrine, and affirmative action. Academic norms require that faculty stand ready to revise their conclusions in the light of new evidence. And experience has shown that faculty members can and do combine strong commitments to a particular point of view with the highest professional standards of teaching and research.

Academic freedom is concerned with protecting the conditions that lead to the creation of sound scholarship and good teaching, not with maintaining political neutrality. Indeed, the Sproul policy's effort to spell out a single criterion that would apply in all disputes over academic freedom was one of its weaknesses. Further, by formulating the issue in political terms, the policy suggested that the University's administration or the governing board should judge whether neutrality had been violated. Such an approach would not be consistent with our current understanding of shared governance, the role of peer review in judging research and teaching, or the division of authority among faculty, administration, and the governing board.

In sum, the Sproul policy is outdated because of its political agenda and because it is insufficiently helpful as a guide for resolving questions of academic freedom. For these reasons, we concluded it should be replaced.

OTHER POLICIES ON ACADEMIC FREEDOM

We began by considering other policies on academic freedom put forth by the AAUP and a number of American universities. Many of these policies conceive of academic freedom, in part, as an extension of First Amendment rights expressed in the U.S. Constitution. However, this conception does not provide a sufficient basis for defining academic freedom. First Amendment rights are about individual freedoms relative to the state. The state cannot tell individual faculty members—or anyone else—that their ideas are wrong or inadequate. However, while the state may not pass judgment on the content of the speech of individual faculty members, universities judge the speech of faculty all the time. Universities award tenure, promotions, and salaries based upon an evaluation of the academic quality of faculty expression. A professor cannot rely on the First Amendment to protect him or her from the judgment of colleagues that his or her research or teaching is professionally inadequate.

The various policies that we reviewed tended to focus on the rights and privileges of a faculty member. Invariably, they inserted a reference to the special obligations and responsibilities of the faculty member. But there was neither clarity about the standard for defining responsibilities nor a procedure for judging whether or not a faculty member met that standard. This matter concerned us, because we believe that a standard of judgment should exist before a crisis or controversy arises.

NEW U.C. POLICY ON ACADEMIC FREEDOM

After concluding that existing policies did not provide an adequate basis for defining academic freedom, we enlisted Professor Robert Post to undertake the responsibility of formulating a new policy for the University. Professor Post is one of the nation's foremost experts on academic freedom, has served as general counsel for the AAUP, and is now a member of the AAUP's Committee on Academic Freedom and Tenure. I asked him, in consultation with Professor Gayle Binion, chair of the U.C. faculty senate, and James Holst, U.C. general counsel, and his associates, David Birnbaum and Steven Rosen, to draft a new policy for consideration.

In a letter dated March 12, 2003, Professor Post conveyed a draft of a three-paragraph academic-freedom policy. That draft has been reviewed and modified by various faculty committees and our general counsel, but its substance is fundamentally unchanged. The revised statement follows:

> The University of California is committed to upholding and preserving principles of academic freedom. These principles reflect the University's fundamental mission, which is to discover knowledge and to disseminate it to its students and to society at large. The principles of academic freedom protect freedom of inquiry and research, freedom of teaching, and freedom of expression and publication. These freedoms enable the University to advance knowledge and its faculty to transmit it effectively to their students and to the public. The University also seeks to foster in its students a mature independence of mind, and this purpose cannot be achieved unless students and faculty are free within the classroom to express the widest range of viewpoints in accord with the standards of scholarly inquiry and professional ethics. The exercise of academic freedom entails correlative duties of professional care when teaching, conducting research, or otherwise acting as a member of the faculty. These duties are set forth in The Faculty Code of Conduct (APM 015).
>
> Academic freedom requires that teaching and scholarship be assessed only by reference to the professional standards that sustain the University's pursuit and achievement of knowledge. The substance and nature of these standards properly lie within the expertise and authority of the faculty as a body. The competence of the faculty to apply these standards of assessment is recognized in the Standing Orders of the Regents, which establish a system of shared governance between the Administration and the Academic Senate. Academic freedom requires

that the Academic Senate be given primary responsibility for applying academic standards, subject to appropriate review by the Administration, and that the Academic Senate exercise its responsibility in full compliance with applicable standards of professional care.

Members of the faculty are entitled as University employees to the full protections of the Constitution of the United States and of the Constitution of the State of California. These protections are in addition to whatever rights, privileges, and responsibilities attach to the academic freedom of university faculty.

The first and third paragraphs of the new policy substantially reflect current understandings of academic freedom expressed most fully in principles proposed by the AAUP. Paragraph two, however, proposes a procedure for assessing the obligations and responsibilities of a faculty member, a procedure that has not been advanced in any of the other policies we have examined.

EXPLANATION OF THE NEW POLICY

The first paragraph begins with the traditional definition of the mission of the university, that of "discovering and disseminating knowledge to our students and to the public." It follows the AAUP statement and refers to the tripartite division of academic freedom derived from this mission: "freedom of inquiry and research, freedom of teaching, and freedom of expression and publication." These freedoms for individual faculty members are part of the AAUP's "General Report of the Committee on Academic Freedom and Tenure" (1915), and are also referenced in the AAUP's 1940 "Statement of Principles on Academic Freedom and Tenure"; they have been widely accepted and endorsed. The right to freedom of expression and publication refers both to the right to speak in public as a scholar and a citizen, and also to speak as a participant in the university's affairs.

In one respect, however, the first paragraph goes beyond the AAUP principles by addressing the relationship between academic freedom and teaching. It states that one essential aspect of faculty teaching is to instill independence of mind in the students. Post, in his letter of transmittal, explained:

> Academic freedom in teaching is sometimes justified solely in terms of the need to disseminate to students the fruits of scholarly research; . . . But in my view academic freedom in teaching also depends on the need to attain the distinct educational objective, characteristic of universities, of fostering in our students the ability to think for themselves as mature adults.

To fulfill this objective, faculty members themselves must have the freedom to model intellectual independence in the classroom. Further, they must create a classroom environment in which students have freedom to express their own perspectives and question those of others without fear of negative consequences for their grades or academic standing.

The third paragraph of the revision makes clear that University faculty enjoy constitutional rights under the Constitution of the United States and the Constitution of the State of California, just as other citizens enjoy such rights.

The second paragraph is where the policy departs from more traditional statements. It addresses the relationship between academic freedom and the professional autonomy of the professoriate. Post explained:

The historical roots of academic freedom lie in this autonomy. The basic idea is that what counts as knowledge, scholarship, and teaching, turns on the application of professional standards of judgment. This idea has many implications. The most important is that the quality of faculty work is to be judged only by reference to professional standards of academic judgment. It is not to be determined by reference to the political decisions of the electorate, the priorities of financial donors, or the managerial priorities of the administration. Academic freedom historically developed in this country precisely because of the need to insulate faculty from these inappropriate bases of judgment.

A second important implication of the idea that the mission of the university depends upon the application of professional standards is that faculty have the responsibility both to assess the work of their peers and also to submit to the assessment of their peers. This responsibility is what underlies decisions concerning hiring, promotion, awarding tenure, approval of course descriptions, evaluations of teaching, and so forth. A third implication is that faculty must undertake to comply with professional standards in the performance of their duties. In the realm of teaching, for example, professional standards require that faculty accord students the right to think freely and to exercise independent judgment; that they evaluate students solely on the merits of their work; and that they not penalize students merely because of their political, ethical, or religious perspectives. If academic freedom implies professional autonomy, it also implies professional responsibility. Academic freedom does not shield faculty from judgment or evaluation if they act in ways that are professionally unethical or incompetent. We specify the nature of the professional responsibility of faculty in §015 of the APM (Faculty Code of Conduct).

This new policy makes clear that academic freedom does not rest principally on the First Amendment rights of individual faculty, nor is it contingent on the sufferance of the state. Rather, academic freedom is rooted in notions of the faculty as members of an academic profession that has distinctive competencies essential to the functioning of the modern university. The faculty, as members of this academic profession, set their own standards governing how knowledge is created, assessed, and advanced.

IMPLICATIONS OF THE NEW POLICY

This new policy does not seek to change in any way the authority of the Board of Regents to govern the University of California, or the responsibility of the administration to perform its appropriate role in governance. It *is* intended to clarify something that has not been explicitly stated in any of the other policies we have examined—namely, that primary responsibility for issues involving academic freedom rests with the faculty. If a faculty member is working on a question germane to his or her discipline and addresses that question in an academically responsible way (adhering to the standards of his or her discipline), the institution has no basis for sanctioning the individual, no matter how controversial that person's viewpoint may be. Still, while the prerogatives of the university are limited, faculty are bound by professional standards and are subject to professional review and sanction. Faculty cannot violate professional standards and defend their conduct on the basis of academic freedom.

The reliance on peer review is fundamentally important. Without peer evaluation, the modern university could not function. Without the freedom to explore within the parameters of academic competence and professional norms, the university could not achieve its mission of advancing knowledge. That is why academic freedom is afforded special protection in American universities. At the same time, the new policy describes how the rights of the faculty are accompanied by broad responsibilities regarding the conduct of teaching and research, the assessment of evidence, and the regard that must be given to alternative viewpoints. Because of their professional expertise and their wide experience with the daily realities of teaching, research, and public service, the faculty have distinctive competencies that make them the most qualified members of the university community to judge on issues of academic freedom.

The new policy has disappointed some people who prefer to see a codification of what behavior is permitted and what is prohibited. I understand this desire. However, we already have a statement governing faculty behavior in APM 015—the Faculty Code of Conduct. The code, for example, forbids discrimination against a student on political grounds; it states:

> As teachers, the professors encourage the free pursuit of learning of their students. They hold before them the best scholarly standards of their discipline. Professors demonstrate respect for students as individuals and adhere to their proper roles as intellectual guides and counselors. Professors make every reasonable effort to foster honest academic conduct and to assure their evaluations of students reflect each student's true merit. . . . They avoid any exploitation, harassment, or discriminatory treatment of students. . . . They protect their academic freedom. (APM 015, Section II.A., p. 4.)

The code sets forth ethical principles and provides examples of unacceptable faculty behaviors that are subject to University discipline. No such list of examples can ever be complete; the code simply illustrates the types of unacceptable conduct that can be derived from the ethical principles.

Our new policy on academic freedom affirms the principle that faculty conduct will be assessed in reference to academic values and professional norms, an inherently broad and flexible standard that is properly left to the determination of the faculty. This articulation of academic freedom implies that the key to proper governance and responsible faculty conduct lies in the careful recruitment and advancement of faculty based on academic values, reliance on faculty to govern themselves wisely, and the expectation that they will fulfill their responsibility to discipline faculty members who violate the norms of the academic profession.

Faculty governance, peer review, and academic freedom gave rise to the research university as we know it today. We would be wise to anticipate that boundaries will change between disciplines, and between the university and other institutions. How research is conducted and how education takes place will change. Sources of support will become more volatile and varied. Professional and political relationships will become more complex. The challenges facing the research university will only expand.

If we wish to meet these challenges wisely and responsibly, we must reaffirm the importance of academic freedom and the accompanying responsibilities of the faculty. This requires that universities rely, not on increasingly elaborate rules and regulations constraining faculty behavior, but rather on the values and norms that must govern faculty professional conduct. This, in turn, requires reaffirmation that modern universities can flourish only when there is a system of shared governance in which faculty are given primary authority, with accompanying freedom and responsibility, over academic matters.

NOTES

An early version of this paper was presented at the Glion Colloquium "Reinventing the Research University," held in Glion, Switzerland, June 2003. The current version was published in the *Proceedings of the American Philosophical Society* vol. 148, no. 2 (June 2004). Reprinted with permission.

A New World of
Scholarly Communication

November 2003

Higher-education leaders invariably have long lists of difficult issues to confront. These days, high on my list is the future of our university libraries. Although libraries form the basic infrastructure of the academic endeavor, I have come face to face with an unhappy fact: University librarians are now being forced to work with faculty members to choose more of the publications they can do *without*. The ballooning costs of academic publications are preventing faculty members and researchers from gaining access to the world's scholarship and knowledge.

Even in the best of economic times, university libraries cannot hope to keep pace with the 6 to 12 percent annual inflation rate in the price of scholarly journals. And the fiscal environment today is particularly difficult—states are facing unprecedented budget crises just as expanding faculties and student bodies are increasing the demand for scholarly information. Neither university librarians nor faculty members alone can deal with the challenges of preserving access to scholarly resources. Presidents must become involved and help lead our institutions into a very different world of scholarly communication.

Higher-education leaders should consider several strategies, including:

DEVELOPING AND SUPPORTING NEW MODELS OF SCHOLARLY PUBLISHING THAT CUT THE COSTS OF DISTRIBUTING AND RETRIEVING INFORMATION

Several organizations are experimenting with less-expensive ways to disseminate faculty research. Some of them are already well known, like JSTOR, which digitally archives more than three hundred journals in various disciplines, and Stanford University's HighWire, which stores online several hundred journals in biology, physics, and other sciences. Others, like BioMed Central and the Public Library of Science in both biology and medicine, are only just emerging. Although it is too soon to know whether any of those services will significantly reduce the cost of scholarly communication or just shift the burden elsewhere, they deserve our support. We can demonstrate that support financially and by explicitly encouraging faculty members to make use of those models.

At the same time, we must not jeopardize the health or well-being of the scholarly societies and university presses that play so critical a role in academic life. Faculty members should continue to manage their intellectual property and copyright. They should decide which publishing organizations they will review, edit, and write for. When signing a publishing contract, they should determine whether to assign the publisher copyright and whether to seek a nonexclusive right to disseminate their work freely in an electronic form.

As they do so, however, faculty members should recognize and reward colleagues who choose alternative ways to disseminate their research. The rapid emergence of scholarly electronic publishing challenges our traditional methods of assessing professors' work for tenure and promotion purposes. We should take steps to guarantee that our evaluation practices keep pace with the adoption of new communication technologies. At the University of California, for instance, the Academic Senate supports consideration of electronic publications in academic peer review.

GIVING FACULTY MEMBERS THE NECESSARY TOOLS TO MAKE THEIR PUBLICATIONS MORE ACCESSIBLE

Universities should shoulder the costs of developing, managing, and publicizing research—including peer review of scholarly papers—and build the online capacity to distribute those works worldwide. The costs, though not insignificant, pale in comparison to those that libraries must bear to buy access to our faculty members' publications.

For example, the University of California, through the California Digital Library's eScholarship program, promotes the wide availability of scholarly works in the arts and humanities, as well as in the social, biomedical, and physical sciences. The Massachusetts Institute of Technology's DSpace initiative has similar cross-disciplinary aims. Cornell University, meanwhile, has taken a subject-based approach through ArXiv.org, an e-print server that supports open-access distribution of scholarship in high-energy physics, mathematics, and related disciplines.

HELPING OUR LIBRARIES POOL THEIR COLLECTION EFFORTS

The alternative—many parallel, redundant research collections—is outmoded and no longer affordable. Our research libraries already collaborate to stretch their dollars. When they bargain collectively with publishers and distributors, they achieve significant savings. When they share print holdings through fast and reliable interlibrary-loan services, they ensure scholars' access to a universe of printed materials larger than any single university library can afford. When they come together to operate cost-effective offsite facilities to store infrequently used materials, they provide affordable access to a richer collection than any one institution can house locally.

Yet our libraries are hampered in their progress. They are rewarded for clinging to their independence, their redundant holdings, and ultimately to strategies that give their patrons a restricted view of the world of scholarly knowledge.

One impediment stands out, if only because it is within our collective ability to remove. The homage that we pay to the Association of Research Libraries' membership index— which ranks the association's more than 120 member libraries largely according to the number of volumes they hold on their shelves—is self-defeating. The index does not count the electronic or print materials that library consortia own and manage, and thus provides no incentive for consortium members to forgo acquiring holdings that are otherwise available to the system as a whole. Even though the membership index rewards inefficiency and waste, we continue to treat it as a meaningful measure.

The association can help by giving credit to its members for building shared collections and for effectively applying technology to their delivery. It should continue to fulfill its historic role, rewarding in rankings those institutions that provide speedy access to, and preserve for posterity, research and teaching material. But in a networked digital age, excessive attention to the local management and ownership of physical materials impedes the responsible stewardship of the scholarly and cultural record.

CLARIFYING WITH FACULTY MEMBERS THE ECONOMIC AND EDUCATIONAL ADVANTAGES OF ALTERNATIVE FORMS OF SCHOLARLY PUBLISHING

We should make sure that they understand how their tens of thousands of individual decisions to produce and use scholarly information ultimately affect our ability to support their research. Libraries need to demonstrate that local maintenance of infrequently consulted print materials undermines, rather than enhances, faculty members' access to research. Money that could be used to add to the breadth of shared collections flows instead toward acquiring and managing duplicative local holdings.

Meanwhile, we should inform faculty members about publishers' pricing structures. We also can disclose information about the very different negotiating stances that publishers take with university libraries over interlibrary loan, preservation, and other conditions that affect how, and at what cost, research information will be available for scholarly use. The system-wide library leadership at the University of California, for instance, has been working with the Academic Senate leadership to mount such an informational campaign for faculty members.

If universities continue to operate as we do now, our library collections will grow—but their scope and depth will diminish precipitously. It is the responsibility of top university leaders to lead the charge for a realistic assessment of how we can head off an otherwise inevitable loss of academic resources.

NOTES

This article was published in the *Chronicle of Higher Education,* November 7, 2003. Copyright © 2003 The Chronicle of Higher Education.

Achievement versus Aptitude

Standardized Tests and Access to American Universities

February 2001

It is a distinct pleasure to present the Robert H. Atwell Distinguished Lecture. I have known and admired Bob for many years. As president of Pitzer College, as head of the American Council on Education, and in many other roles as well, he has been an eloquent voice on behalf of the nation's colleges and universities, and for that we are all in his debt. I cannot think of a better way to recognize his important contributions than by this annual lecture in his honor.

More than any other country in the world, the United States has sought to put a college education within the reach of anyone with the talent and determination to succeed. And we have tried to allocate educational opportunity in ways that reflect American ideals of fairness and egalitarianism. Many argue that the use of standardized tests in admissions, and particularly the SAT, promotes those ideals by providing a common measure of readiness for college-level study. I have reached a very different conclusion, and that is what I want to talk about today.

A PROPOSAL

Recently, I asked the Academic Senate of the University of California to consider two major changes in our admissions policies. First, I recommended that the University require only standardized tests that assess mastery of specific subject areas rather than undefined notions of aptitude or intelligence. To facilitate this change, I recommended that we no longer require the SAT I for students applying to U.C. This recommendation has significant implications for the University of California, since we are one of the principal users of the SAT.

Second, I recommended that all campuses move away from admissions processes that use narrowly defined quantitative formulas, and instead adopt procedures that look at applicants in a comprehensive way. While this recommendation is intended to provide a fairer basis on which to make admissions decisions, it would also help ensure that standardized tests do not have an undue influence but rather are used to illuminate the student's total record.

In the short term, these proposals will not result in earth-shaking changes in determining which students are admitted and which are rejected. In the long term, however, they will help strengthen high school curricula and pedagogy, create a stronger connection between what students accomplish in high school and their likelihood of being admitted to U.C., and focus student attention on mastery of subject matter rather than test preparation. These changes will help all

students, especially low-income and minority students, determine their own educational destinies. And they will lead to
greater public confidence in the fairness of the University of
California's admissions process.

Further, these changes will complement K-12 reform efforts
that have been launched in California and around the nation to
establish clear curricular guidelines, set high academic standards,
and employ standardized tests to assess student achievement.

Let me describe how I came to make these recommendations. For many years, I have worried about the use of the SAT,
but last year my concerns coalesced. I visited an upscale private
school and observed a class of twelve-year-old students studying
verbal analogies in anticipation of the SAT. I learned that they
spend hours each month—directly and indirectly—preparing
for the SAT, studying long lists of verbal analogies such as "un-
truthful is to mendaciousness as circumspect is to caution." The
time involved was not aimed at developing the students' reading and writing abilities but rather their test-taking skills. What
I saw was disturbing and prompted me to spend time taking
sample SAT tests and reviewing the literature. I concluded what
many others have concluded—that America's overemphasis on
the SAT is compromising our educational system.

OVEREMPHASIS ON STANDARDIZED TESTS

Let me make clear that I continue to be a strong supporter of
standardized tests. I have high regard for the Educational Testing Service [ETS], which produces the SAT. Its staff knows how
to develop and evaluate tests and has an excellent record of administering tests and ensuring security. My concern is not with

the ability of ETS to develop and administer standardized tests but with the appropriateness of the SAT in college admissions.

Developed properly and used responsibly, standardized tests can help students gauge their progress and help the general public assess the effectiveness of schools. The problem is not the use of standardized tests to assess knowledge in well-defined subject areas. The problem is tests that do not have a demonstrable relationship to the student's program of study—a problem that is amplified when the tests are assumed to measure innate ability.

Many students spend a great deal of time preparing for the SAT. But students are not the only ones affected. Nobody is spared—not teachers, not parents, not admissions officers, not university presidents.

Teachers, knowing that they will be judged by the scores their students make, are under pressure to teach to the test. College admissions officers are under pressure to increase the SAT scores of each entering class. They know that their president, faculty, and alumni pay attention to how SAT scores affect their standing in college rankings, like those published by *U.S. News & World Report*. The stakes are so high that nobody is surprised when the *Wall Street Journal* reports that some universities manipulate—and indeed falsify—SAT scores in an effort to attain a higher ranking.

Knowing how important the SAT is in the admissions game, some parents go to great lengths to help their children get high scores. The *Los Angeles Times* reported that a growing number of affluent parents shop around for a psychologist willing to certify that their child is learning disabled so he or she can qualify for extra time on the SAT.

Many parents who can afford the fees enroll their children in SAT preparation courses. Last year alone, an estimated one hundred fifty thousand students paid over one hundred million dollars for coaching provided by the Princeton Review, Stanley Kaplan, and the like.

Given the attempts of some individuals and institutions to gain any advantage, fair or foul, is it any wonder that leaders of minority communities perceive the SAT to be unfair? These concerns are often dismissed as sour grapes, as special "ethnic pleading." The response by defenders of the SAT is, "Don't shoot the messenger." They argue that the lower performance of blacks and Hispanics reflects the fact that blacks and Hispanics tend to be clustered in poor schools, offering outdated curricula taught by ill-prepared teachers.

Minority perceptions about fairness cannot be so easily dismissed. Of course, minorities are concerned about the fact that, on average, their children score lower than white and Asian American students. The real basis of their concern, however, is that they have no way of knowing what the SAT measures and, therefore, have no basis for assessing its fairness or helping their children acquire the skills to do better.

Most troubling of all, SAT scores can have a profound effect on how students regard themselves. All of us have known students who excelled in high school, students who did everything expected of them and more, who suddenly doubt their accomplishments, their abilities, and their basic worth because they scored poorly on the SAT.

Anyone involved in education should be concerned about how overemphasis on the SAT is distorting educational priorities and practices, how the test is perceived by many as unfair, and how it can have a devastating impact on the self-esteem and aspirations of young students. However, while there is widespread agreement that overemphasis on the SAT harms American education, there is no consensus on what to do or where to start. In many ways, we are caught up in the educational equivalent of a nuclear arms race. We know that this overemphasis on test scores hurts all involved, especially students. But we also know that anyone or any institution opting out of the competition does so at considerable risk.

Change is long overdue. Accordingly, I am recommending that U.C. change its test requirements in the admissions process.

EVOLUTION OF THE SAT

Let me place my comments in perspective with some observations about how the SAT has evolved over the years. Originally, the test was developed to serve a distinctly American purpose. The College Board first met in 1900 and held its first examinations in spring 1901. The goals of these exams were: (a) to move away from the existing system, in which each university had its own examination (of unknown validity, and if students wanted to apply to several universities, they had to take one exam per university); (b) to provide feedback to secondary schools about what should be covered in their curricula and the appropriate level of instruction (i.e., standards); and (c) to widen the net of student applicants (at the time, prep schools provided certificates for some students, which served as the entry hurdle for others). The initial tests of the College Board were clearly achievement tests with no implication that they measured "innate intelligence." They were intended to serve an egalitarian purpose. They were designed to identify students from a wide range of backgrounds who had demonstrated mastery of academic subjects needed to succeed in college.

But this changed in the 1930s. The then-president of Harvard University, James Conant, wanted to make the SAT a test not of achievement, but of basic aptitude. His motivations were good. He wanted to reduce the advantage that wealthy students enjoyed by virtue of having attended schools with a rich curriculum and excellent teachers. However well intentioned, this change brought with it a sense that the SAT was akin to an IQ test—a measure of innate intelligence.

The College Board has since made attempts to change this perception. In 1990, it changed the name of the SAT from Scholastic Aptitude Test to Scholastic Assessment Test. And in 1996, it dropped the name altogether and said that the SAT was the SAT and that the initials no longer stood for anything. Rather than resolving the problem, this rhetorical sleight of hand served to underscore the mystery of what the SAT is supposed to measure.

Many universities, faced with the problem of having to choose from among thousands of highly qualified applicants, have adopted practices that give too much weight to the SAT. College presidents and others have candidly acknowledged that, while they appreciate the limitations of the test, they continue to rely on SAT scores because they provide a convenient basis for justifying admission decisions.

All too often, universities use SAT scores to rank order applicants in determining who should be admitted. This use of the SAT is not compatible with the American view on how merit should be defined and opportunities distributed. The strength of American society has been its belief that actual achievement should be what matters most. Students should be judged on the basis of what they have made of the opportunities available to them. In other words, in America, students should be judged on what they have accomplished during four years of high school, taking into account their opportunities.

THE CALIFORNIA CONUNDRUM

The University of California requires that high school students take a set of college-preparatory courses—ranging from English, social sciences, and foreign languages to mathematics and a laboratory science. Those required courses shape the high school curriculum in direct and powerful ways. Under the California Master Plan for Higher Education, students who compile an academic record placing them among the top 12½ percent statewide of high school seniors are guaranteed a space at one of the U.C. campuses.

U.C. draws its students from over one thousand comprehensive public and private high schools around the state. These schools vary widely in terms of the quality of faculty and curriculum. As elsewhere in the nation, low-income and minority students tend to be concentrated in poorer schools, with a limited curriculum taught by a large percentage of underprepared teachers.

U.C. has a particularly difficult responsibility to fulfill. As the public institution entrusted by the state to educate its top high school graduates, it must set high standards. At the same time, U.C. must set standards that are attainable by individual students attending any of the state's comprehensive high schools. U.C. must also be mindful that it serves the most racially and ethnically diverse college-going population in the nation. The University must be careful to make sure that its standards do not unfairly discriminate against any students.

U.C. campuses have historically balanced these imperatives by giving the most weight to high school grades in the college preparatory courses required for U.C. admission. In this way, campuses attempt to strike a balance between meritocratic and egalitarian values. The criteria are meritocratic in that they emphasize grades earned in demanding courses. The criteria are egalitarian in that, in theory, they can be met by any student attending any high school in the state. However, because grading standards vary from high school to high school, we need some form of standardized testing and have in the past turned to the SAT.

When faced with large numbers of students applying for relatively few spots, admissions officers, unless they are very careful, will give undue weight to the SAT. All U.C. campuses have tried to ensure that SAT scores are used properly in the admissions process. However, because California's college-age population will grow by 50 percent over the next decade and become even more diverse than it is today, additional steps must be taken now to ensure that test scores are kept in proper perspective.

RECOMMENDATIONS

I have recommended that the faculty adopt the following criteria when setting requirements for standardized tests.

· The academic competencies to be tested should be clearly defined. There should be a demonstrable relationship between what is tested and what the student studied in high school. In other words, testing should be directly related to the required college preparatory curriculum.

· Students from any comprehensive high school in California should be able to score well if they mastered the curriculum.

· Students should be able to review their score and understand where they did well or fell short and what they must do to earn higher scores in the future.

· Test scores should help admissions officers evaluate the applicant's readiness for college-level work.

Let me now turn to specific recommendations. Henceforth, I will no longer refer to the SAT in general, but to the SAT I and the SAT II, and will assume that you are familiar with these two tests.[1] Based on the criteria listed above, I have proposed that the faculty adopt the following changes in the admissions process.

· No longer require that students take the SAT I in order to apply for admission to the University.

· Call for the development of standardized tests that are directly tied to the college preparatory courses required of students applying to U.C.

· Until these tests are available, continue to require the SAT II. Under current U.C. admissions policy, applicants are required to take three SAT II subject tests, namely, writing, mathematics, and a third test of their choice.

· Establish policies and guidelines governing the use of standardized tests. In particular, make sure that tests are not overvalued, but rather used to illuminate other aspects of a student's record.

The SAT II begins to approximate what I judge to be an appropriate test for the University's admissions process. It tests students on specific subjects that are well defined and readily described. Of course, it is not coordinated with U.C.-required college preparatory courses, but at least students and their families know what to expect.

For some years, U.C. has required both the SAT I and the SAT II. Because U.C. enrolls a large number of students and has required tests for many years, we have the data necessary to make judgments about the value of different tests in our admissions process. We know that high school grades are by far the best predictor of first-year college performance. We have also found that the SAT II is a better predictor of performance than the SAT I. Further, the SAT II augmented by the SAT I is only slightly better than the SAT II alone in predicting freshman grades.

COMPREHENSIVE REVIEWS

Changing standardized test requirements is a step in the right direction, but in the best of circumstances there will be a tendency to overemphasize test scores. Admissions officers at U.C. campuses recognize this problem and have introduced more comprehensive evaluation processes. Included in the comprehensive evaluation is the quality of the high school and the environment in which the student was raised. A student who has made exceptional progress in troubled circumstances needs to be given special attention.

These comprehensive procedures have been well received by the public. Students report that they appreciate review processes that look at the full range of their accomplishments within the context of the opportunities they enjoyed and the obstacles they faced.

CONCLUSION

These proposed changes in U.C.'s admissions process will come at some cost. They are labor intensive and therefore expensive. However, considering the importance of admissions decisions to individual students and to society at large, we have no choice but to invest the necessary funds.

If the Academic Senate responds favorably to these recommendations, then U.C. would reaffirm its commitment to assessing achievement in ways appropriate to the twenty-first century—a commitment to assess students in their full complexity. Such decisions are difficult because they involve making sense of grades earned in different courses taught at very different schools. They require that judgments be made about the opportunities available to individual students. They call on admissions officers to look into the future and make judgments about what individual applicants might contribute to campus life and, later, to society. These are extraordinarily tough decisions that require both wisdom and humility. But the stakes are too high not to ensure that the job is done right.

NOTES

These remarks were delivered as the 2001 Robert H. Atwell Distinguished Lecture at the 83rd Annual Meeting of the American Council on Education, Washington, D.C., February 18, 2001.

1. The SAT IIs are individual tests designed to measure knowledge in specific subject areas. The SAT I, in contrast, focuses on verbal and mathematical abilities that are used to help predict first-year college grades.

The California Crucible:
Demography, Excellence, and Access
at the University of California

July 2001

Last February I gave an address to the American Council on Education about two proposals I have made to the Academic Senate of the University of California. The first proposal was that the University make the SAT I examination optional for admission to the University of California, and that we replace it with a standardized test that assesses mastery of specific academic subject areas rather than aptitude, as the SAT I purports to do. The second was that the University should move away from admissions processes that use narrowly defined quantitative formulas and, instead, adopt procedures that look at applicants in a more comprehensive way.

In California, admissions issues inspire the kind of passion that in England or Italy is reserved for the World Cup. The reasons are similar: those involved know that it is a high-stakes game, that not everyone can play, and that the winners can count on substantial rewards. But I was unprepared for the national response to my proposal. I have heard from hundreds of educators, students, parents, and members of the public from around the country, many with moving personal stories about their experience with the SAT I. Clearly, a national debate on the SAT I and its influence on the lives and prospects of millions of American young people is overdue.

Yet reactions to my proposal have also made it clear that there is some confusion about what I proposed and why I proposed it. Many do not realize, for example, that eliminating the SAT I as a requirement is only one of several admissions changes I have recommended to the Academic Senate.

Today, I would like to describe the context of my several proposals and the reasons I consider them steps in the right direction for the University. To understand why admissions issues at the University of California are the focus of so much public attention in this state, you have to understand some things about California.

A DIVERSE AND KNOWLEDGE-DRIVEN SOCIETY

California is one of the nation's first "new societies"—a society in which no racial or ethnic group predominates. With thirty-four million people, California is not only the nation's most populous state; it is also the most diverse. One in every four Californians was born outside the United States. It is estimated that by 2005, one in every three Californians will be foreign born. Native Mexicans constitute 44 percent of California's immigrants; another 10 percent come from other

Latin American countries; and Asians make up 34 percent of the state's newcomers. Nearly four in ten Californians speak a language other than English at home. Although the biggest population increases in recent decades have been among the state's Hispanics and Asians, more than sixty different countries, from Australia to Yugoslavia, contribute immigrants to California. No other state—and no other country—has the range of races, ethnicities, languages, and cultures that characterize California today.

And to glimpse California's future, look at the composition of the nearly six million children enrolled in its K-12 public schools. Forty-three percent are Hispanic and 36 percent are white. Asians and Pacific Islanders make up 11 percent, while African Americans number close to 9 percent and Native Americans are just under 1 percent. Twenty percent of these students have limited proficiency in English.

The demands on California's public schools are staggering. Their quality ranges from schools that can compare with the best in the nation to schools in which literacy is the ceiling rather than the floor of student achievement. The state's governor, Gray Davis, has made school reform the principal priority of his administration and has asked the University to play a significant role in improving the academic preparation of *all* California students. The University of California is spending well over three hundred million dollars a year to improve public schooling and to increase access to higher education. Our professional-development programs in reading and algebra help seventy thousand teachers a year; our counseling and academic support programs reach over one hundred thousand students and families; and each of our campuses is involved in long-term partnerships with public schools—all together, over three hundred elementary, middle, and high schools.

The students who apply to U.C. come from public and private high schools around the state that vary widely in terms of the quality of teaching and curricula, opportunities to take advanced placement courses, and even the availability of basic textbooks. The students themselves come from communities that range from extreme poverty to great affluence, from the rural Central Valley to urban Los Angeles. Some have parents who enroll them in preschool and later hire tutors to help them with algebra; some struggle to learn in schools with crumbling classrooms and teachers who are overworked and underprepared. These students have vastly different lives and dramatically different opportunities to learn.

California is not only a highly diverse society; it is also a premier example of an economy driven by knowledge. The state has some eighty thousand scientists and engineers, the largest concentration in the country. California institutions were issued more than eighteen thousand patents in 1999—20 percent of all U.S. patents issued that year. Many of those patents went to scientists and engineers at U.C., which earns more patents annually than any other educational institution.

California's public and private sectors expended over forty-two billion dollars on research in 1997—more than the next three highest states combined. Everyone has heard of Silicon Valley; it is less well known that Southern California produces almost 40 percent of California's high-technology goods and services. Innovation is as much a part of the California landscape as freeways and palm trees.

The critical role of innovation and research in the California economy has been well demonstrated. Huge cuts in the aerospace and defense industries sent the state into a devastating recession in the early 1990s. Those jobs have never been replaced, but hundreds of new high-technology companies, fueled by technologies created at California's research universities, have made up for all the jobs we lost *and* created thousands of additional high-paying jobs. Computer software, biotechnology, telecommunications, and other knowledge-intensive industries are driving the California economy today. It is widely recognized that the state's excellent system of higher education, especially its research universities, has been a key advantage in California's rise to the fifth-largest economy in the world.

The state expects the University of California to contribute the innovative research on which our knowledge-based economy depends. We are able to do so because of the distinction of our faculty and the size of our research enterprise. Recognizing the enormous contributions University research makes to economic growth, Governor Davis has established four California Institutes for Science and Innovation. The purpose of these institutes is to create the knowledge-based industries of the future, and they involve a partnership among U.C., state government, and more than two hundred of the state's high-technology businesses. Each institute will focus on areas of multidisciplinary research critical to the California economy—biomedicine, bioengineering, nanosystems, telecommunications, and information technology. The institutes will also help produce the next generation of scientists and engineers by giving undergraduate and graduate students the opportunity to involve themselves in research with some of the state's best minds from both industry and academia.

EXCELLENCE AND ACCESS

California is clear about the role it expects the University to play in making this diverse and knowledge-driven society work. We must contribute cutting-edge research to fuel the state's economy and provide an education for the state's citizens that combines excellence and access. I have already discussed U.C.'s research role. Now let me turn to education.

California is unique in promising access to the state's public colleges and universities to every citizen with the ability and motivation to succeed. We need broad access to prepare students for the responsibilities of citizenship in a society where so many cultures, languages, and traditions intersect. And in a knowledge-based economy like California's, life is much kinder to the skilled than the unskilled. Someone with a bachelor's degree can expect to earn almost 70 percent more over a working lifetime than someone with only a high school diploma. As a public university, we are responsible for ensuring that we are open to students from every background and that we recognize intellectual talent in all its many varieties.

Excellence and access are difficult to achieve under any circumstances. They are all the more difficult given that U.C., like California, is growing rapidly. Over the next decade we expect our enrollments to expand by 52,700 students, from 158,300 to 211,000. To keep up with this growth and replace faculty who have retired, we will need to hire seven thousand faculty over the next decade. When you are faced with the need to expand so much and so quickly, the temptation is to lower standards. That would be a strategy for disaster. The University's tradition of faculty excellence must be maintained if we are going to meet our responsibilities to California.

ADMISSIONS POLICIES THAT ARE INCLUSIVE AND FAIR: FOUR PROPOSALS

Now let me explain what all this has to do with admissions policy and the SAT. Under California's Master Plan for Higher Education, the University of California is required to draw its freshman class from the top 12½ percent statewide of high school seniors. We must do so under certain constraints. For example, we cannot use race or ethnicity as factors in admissions, as a result of the passage of Proposition 209 in 1996. Since most U.C. campuses receive far more applications than they can accept, we know that our admissions policies and practices will attract attention not only inside the University but outside as well—from legislators, educators, parents, and students. Every eligible student is guaranteed a place at the University, but not necessarily at the campus of first choice. For the fall of 2001, U.C. received almost ninety-two thousand freshman and transfer applications for thirty-nine thousand places.

To meet its responsibilities to a diverse and knowledge-based society, the University of California must choose the state's highest-performing students in ways that are inclusive and fair. More, they must be *demonstrably* inclusive and fair.

We should do this, in my view, by assessing students in their full complexity, which means considering not only grades and test scores but also what students have made of their opportunities to learn, the obstacles they have overcome, and the special talents they possess. I have made four proposals that seek to move the University in this direction. They are (1) comprehensive review of applicants; (2) Eligibility in the Local Context; (3) Dual Admissions; and (4) changes in test requirements, including the SAT I. I would like to describe each briefly.

Comprehensive Review

Current U.C. policy defines two tiers for admission, and in the first tier students are admitted by a formula that places principal weight on grades and test scores. Selective private universities have by and large used a comprehensive review of a student's full record in making admissions decisions, and given the intense competition for places at U.C., I believe we must follow their lead. I have recommended eliminating the two-tier system in favor of ensuring that every applicant receives the same comprehensive review of his or her achievements and potential. The proposal is now before the Academic Senate, which expects to act on it sometime during the coming fall quarter.

Eligibility in the Local Context

For the first time this year, students can qualify for admission to the University through what we are calling Eligibility in the Local Context, or the Four Percent Plan. This program grants U.C. eligibility to students who are in the top 4 percent of the graduating class in each California high school and who have successfully completed U.C.'s required college-preparatory courses. It ensures that high-performing students, including those from rural and urban schools, have access to U.C. regardless of whether their schools offer such academic enrichment opportunities as advanced placement or honors courses. Almost 97 percent of California public high schools participated in the Four Percent Plan this year, many of which have traditionally sent few or no students to U.C. The response has been enthusiastic from schools and students alike.

Dual Admissions

Another new path to U.C. is the Dual Admissions Proposal, which has been approved by the Academic Senate and will go to the University's Board of Regents for final action later this month. Under the proposal, students who fall below the top 4 percent but within the top 12½ percent of each California high school graduating class would be admitted simultaneously to a community college and to U.C., with the proviso that students must fulfill their freshman and sophomore requirements at the community college with a solid grade-point average before transferring to a U.C. campus. Consistent with Proposition 209, the Dual Admissions Proposal will not admit students based on race or ethnicity. But a large number of students who would qualify under this proposal are Latino, African American, and Native American. Like the Four Percent Plan, the Dual Admissions Proposal, if approved, will give students who have excelled academically in disadvantaged high schools a clear path to a U.C. degree.

Changes in Test Requirements

And this brings me to the last of the proposed changes in U.C. admissions policies. The SAT I—a two-part test assessing mathematical and verbal aptitude—has become the single most influential test in American higher education. Yet as an aptitude test that claims to assess quantitative reasoning and verbal ability, it is based on questionable assumptions about the nature of intelligence. As a rite of passage that can have lasting consequences for the futures of millions of young people every year, it has become a destructive national obsession.

Some have assumed that, because I oppose the SAT I, I also oppose all standardized tests. That is not the case. Grading practices vary across high schools, and standardized tests are essential to providing a measure of what students know that is independent of grades. But we need to be exceedingly careful about which standardized tests we choose. Students should not be judged on the basis of tests that embody ill-defined notions of aptitude or intelligence.

Accordingly, I have recommended that the University make significant changes in its test requirements. Under current U.C. admissions policy, applicants are required to take five tests: the two SAT I aptitude tests and three SAT II achievement tests— writing, mathematics, and a third in a subject of their choice. I have proposed that U.C. no longer require the SAT I for admission but instead use tests that have a demonstrable relationship to the curriculum that students study in preparation for college-level work.

U.C. requires students to take college preparatory courses that are referred to as the "a-g requirements." These requirements cover five main subject areas: English, mathematics, history and social science, laboratory science, and a foreign language. The development of new standardized tests to cover these five areas should not be a difficult task; I believe either the ETS or the ACT could readily accomplish such an assignment for U.C.

Until such tests are developed, the faculty committee responsible for U.C. admissions is considering, among other options, the use of five SAT II tests to replace the two SAT I tests and the three SAT II tests currently required. The five tests would be selected so that they correlated with the a-g requirements.

The principal claim about the usefulness of the SAT I—that it functions as the gold standard of student quality—rests on its supposed capacity to tell us how students will do in their first year of college. As one of the nation's largest users of SAT tests, U.C. is perhaps the only university in the country that has a database large enough to compare the predictive power of the SAT I with that of the achievement-based SAT II tests. We have required both the SAT I and the SAT II since 1968, which means that we can compare component test scores with subsequent college performance for a large pool of students.

These data challenge the conventional wisdom about the superior predictive power of the SAT I. They indicate that the best single predictor of first-year college grades is high school grades; further, the three SAT II tests combined are a far better predictor than the two SAT I tests. If high school grades and the SAT II are combined, then one can account for 22.2 percent of the variance in college freshman grades. Combining high school grades, the SAT II, *and* the SAT I, one can account for 22.3 percent of the variance. In other words, the SAT I adds virtually nothing to our ability to predict freshman college grades.

There is another reason why the SAT I does not serve either students or schools. School reform efforts in California, like others across the country, are based on three principal tenets: curriculum content and goals should be clearly defined; students should be held to well-defined standards; and standardized tests should be used to assess whether those standards have been met. The SAT I, because it is not aligned with subject or scholarship requirements, sends a confusing message to students, teachers, and schools. It says that students will be tested on material that is unrelated to what they study in their classes. It says that the grades they achieve can be devalued by tests of material that is not part of their school curriculum. Most important, the SAT I scores only tell a student that he or she scored higher or lower than his or her classmates. They provide no basis for self-assessment and improvement.

The irony of the SAT I is that it began as an effort to move higher education closer to egalitarian values. Yet its roots are in a very different tradition: the IQ testing that took place during the First World War, when two million men were tested and assigned an IQ based on the results. The framers of these tests assumed that intelligence was a unitary, inherited attribute, that it was not subject to change over a lifetime, and that it could be measured and individuals ranked and assigned their place in society accordingly. Although the SAT I is more sophisticated from a psychometric standpoint, it is based on the same questionable assumptions about human talent and potential. The SAT I gives credence to the notion that intellectual ability is a unidimensional attribute that can be measured and expressed by a single number. I hope California will take a more thoughtful approach.

FINAL REMARKS

The common link among the admissions proposals I have made is that they call on students to work hard and strive for high academic achievement, and in return they commit U.C. to viewing those achievements in the context of the opportunities students enjoyed and the challenges they faced. While these proposals benefit all students, they particularly benefit hardworking, high-achieving students who through no fault of their own attend low-performing schools. In this respect, these proposals complement the educational reform efforts launched by Governor Davis.

The University of California has always reviewed its admissions policies from time to time to ensure that they are right for the young people of this state. The difference between the California of an earlier time and the California of today is that our economy is far more reliant on the generation and application of knowledge, the students coming to us are far more diverse, and the K-12 public schools are far more variable in the quality of their teaching and curricula. What we expect of our students in 2001 is no less rigorous than what we expected in the past. But now the admissions policies we employ to judge student achievement and promise must be comprehensive enough to recognize talent in all its forms. These policies must tell schools what we expect them to teach to prepare students for university-level study. They must give students the message that, with hard work in demanding courses, a University of California education is within their reach. They must help the University do what we have always done, which is to combine excellence and access by setting high standards and admitting students who meet those standards. We have no more important responsibility in the new society that is being born in California today.

NOTES

These remarks were delivered as the keynote address at the 2001 International Assembly of the Council for Advancement and Support of Education, San Francisco, July 2, 2001.

Statement on the Vote by the College Board Trustees to Revise the SAT I

June 2002

I am delighted by the College Board's decision to alter the SAT I examination. It marks a major event in the history of standardized testing. I give enormous credit to the College Board and to its president, Gaston Caperton, for the vision they have demonstrated in bringing forward these changes and for their genuine commitment to improved educational attainment in our nation. By their action today, they have laid the foundation for a new test that will better serve our students and schools.

Standardized tests perform a necessary function in American education, providing a common measure of student performance in an educational system marked by vast disparities between schools. But we need standardized tests that bear a demonstrable relationship to what students actually study in the high school college-preparatory curriculum. We also need to focus student attention on mastery of subject matter rather than mastery of test-taking skills.

The new College Board test will do an excellent job of fulfilling these goals. It will draw on state and national curriculum surveys to establish a clear link between what students are taught in school and what they are tested on for college admission. It will ask students to express their thinking in writing—a critical skill for success in college and beyond—and will focus attention on the teaching of writing in the K-12 schools. It will cover a greater portion of the mathematics curriculum that college-bound students are expected to master. And it has the potential to offer students, parents, and schools more useful feedback about each student's preparation for college-level work.

Some will argue that the improvements adopted by the College Board today do not go far enough. I believe, however, that the College Board has taken the appropriate steps with these reforms. They encourage students to take challenging courses in high school, knowing that their efforts will be reflected in their test scores. In addition, the new test will reinforce K-12 improvement efforts designed to establish clear curricular expectations, set high academic standards, and use standardized tests to assess performance relative to those standards.

At the University of California, the Academic Senate has asked its Board of Admissions and Relations with Schools (BOARS) to continue its collaborative work with both the College Board and ACT, Inc., on the development of admissions tests that reflect the specifications outlined by BOARS earlier this year. That work will continue over the coming months. I thank the Academic Senate for the contribution it has made to the national testing discussion and look forward to our continuing dialogue with both the College Board and ACT.

College Admissions and the SAT:
A Personal Perspective

April 2004

My intent in this paper is to offer a personal perspective on the events that led to a major change in the college admissions test known as the SAT. The new test will be in place for all students—nationwide—who must take the SAT as part of the admissions process for the college class entering in the fall of 2006. Hopefully, this account will be useful to those trying to change policies and practices deeply entrenched in our society.

Before I begin, let me introduce some terminology. By the term *standardized test,* I mean simply a test administered under controlled conditions and carefully monitored to prevent cheating. I will also use the terms *aptitude test* and *achievement test.* Achievement tests are designed to measure mastery of a specific subject. In contrast, aptitude tests are designed to predict an individual's ability to profit from a particular type of training or instruction. For example, an algebra test given at the end of a course would be classified as an achievement test, whereas a test given prior to the course—designed to predict the student's performance in the algebra course—would be classified as an aptitude test. In actual practice, the distinction between achievement and aptitude tests is not as neat as these definitions might suggest, but the conceptual difference is useful.

After World War II, colleges and universities in the United States gradually adopted standardized tests as part of their admissions process. The test that was most widely selected was the Scholastic Aptitude Test, known as the SAT. Some schools used the American College Testing program [ACT], but most institutions, particularly the more selective ones, chose the SAT.

The College Board (the nonprofit organization that owns the SAT) has made a series of changes in the test since its inception. The original SAT became the SAT I—a three-hour test that continued to focus on verbal aptitude but added a quantitative section covering mathematical topics typically taught in grades one through eight. In addition, the College Board developed twenty-three one-hour SAT II tests designed to measure a student's achievement in specific subjects such as physics, chemistry, history, mathematics, writing, and foreign languages. Most colleges and universities required just the SAT I, but some required the SAT I plus two or three SAT II tests.

Today, when the SAT is mentioned in the media, the reference is invariably to the SAT I. The test has become a key factor in determining who is admitted—and who is rejected—at the more selective institutions.

My concerns about the SAT date back to the late 1940s, when I was an undergraduate at the University of Chicago. Many of the Chicago faculty were outspoken critics of the SAT and viewed it as nothing more than a multiple-choice version of an IQ test; they argued forcefully for achievement tests in the college-admissions process. Their opposition may have been influenced to some degree by school rivalry: the leading force behind the SAT at that time was James B. Conant, the president of Harvard University. Eventually, Chicago adopted the SAT, but not without controversy.

In the years after leaving the University of Chicago, I followed the debates about the SAT and IQ tests with great interest. I knew that Carl Brigham, a psychologist at Princeton who created the original SAT, modeled the test after earlier IQ tests and regarded it as a measure of innate mental ability. But years later he expressed doubts about the validity of the SAT and worried that preparing for the test distorted the educational experience of high school students. Harvard's President Conant also expressed serious reservations about the test later in his life. When students asked me about IQ testing, I frequently referred them to Stephen Jay Gould's book *The Mismeasure of Man,* published in 1981. It is a remarkable piece of scholarship that documented the widespread misuse of IQ tests. I knew both Dick Herrnstein at Harvard and Art Jensen at U.C. Berkeley personally and kept track of their controversial work on IQ. And, of course, I was a long-term member of the faculty at Stanford University, where the Stanford-Binet Intelligence Scales were developed.

Over the intervening years, my views about IQ testing proved to be mixed. In the hands of a trained clinician, tests like the Wechsler Intelligence Scales or the Stanford-Binet Intelligence Scales are useful instruments in the diagnosis of learning problems; they can often identify someone with potential who, for whatever reason, is failing to live up to that potential. However, such tests do not have the necessary validity or reliability to justify ranking individuals of normal intelligence, let alone to make fine judgments among highly talented individuals. My views are similar to those of Alfred Binet, the French psychologist who, in the early years of the last century, devised the first IQ tests. Binet was very clear that these tests could be useful in a clinical setting, but he rejected the idea that they provided a meaningful measure of mental ability that could be used to rank order individuals. Unfortunately, his perspective was soon forgotten as the IQ testing industry burst onto the American scene.

So much for my personal history before I became seriously involved with the SAT. My involvement began in the early 1990s, when I served as chair of BOTA, the Board on Testing and Assessment. BOTA is a board of the National Research Council charged with advising the federal government on issues of testing and assessment. BOTA has done a tremendous service, integrating and interpreting research findings in order to advise the government on a wide range of testing and assessment problems for virtually every federal agency.

Serving on BOTA focused my attention on college admissions tests and their effects on a student's high school education and subsequent career. However, the defining moment for me occurred at a meeting of BOTA in Washington, D.C., where representatives of the College Board and the Educational Testing Service [ETS] presented their views on college admissions tests. I left that meeting less than satisfied. The College Board and ETS have a superb record both on the technical aspects of test development and on administering tests and ensuring their security. But at that meeting, the notion that the SAT I was a true measure of intelligence dominated their perspective. Further, they seemed oblivious to several studies suggesting that achievement tests were a better predictor of college success than aptitude tests.

On my way home I stopped in Florida to visit my grandchildren. I found my granddaughter, then in sixth grade, already diligently preparing for the SAT by testing herself on long lists of verbal analogies. She had a corpus of quite obscure words to memorize, and then she proceeded to construct analogies using the words. I was amazed at the amount of time and effort involved, all in anticipation of the SAT. Was this how I wanted my granddaughter to spend her study time?

On the plane trip back to California I drafted an op-ed piece about college admissions tests. It was not focused on the University of California but on college admissions in general. It made a series of points. One was that admissions tests should not try to measure innate intelligence (whatever that is), but should focus on achievement—what the student actually learned during the high school years. In addition, such tests should have an essay component requiring the student to produce an actual writing sample. And the tests should cover more mathematics than simply an eighth-grade introduction to algebra.

And, finally, I said that an important aspect of admissions tests was to convey to students, as well as their teachers and parents, the importance of learning to write and the necessity of mastering at least eighth- through tenth-grade mathematics.

The draft op-ed piece was handwritten. I shared it with a few close friends, decided that the time was not right to raise the issue, and placed it in my desk drawer. But later, when the

SAT controversy erupted, a reporter learned of the draft and requested it under the Freedom of Information Act. To my chagrin, the U.C. general counsel declared that it was a University document and had to be turned over to the reporter.

When I was asked to give the keynote address at the annual meeting of the American Council of Education [ACE] in February 2001, a colleague of mine at the [U.C.] Office of the President, Pat Hayashi, suggested that we use the op-ed draft as the basis for the speech. Pat had been the admissions officer at U.C. Berkeley for a number of years and at the time was serving on the Board of Trustees of the College Board. He has been an important influence on my thinking about admissions issues in general and the SAT in particular.

Although as U.C. president I already had plenty of controversies to contend with, I liked Pat's suggestion, and we proceeded to redo the op-ed piece, but this time focused on the University of California. (The speech can be found at the U.C. Office of the President Web site.)[1] I won't go into the details of the ACE speech. In a nutshell, I said that I intended to recommend to the faculty that the University cease using the SAT I and rely on SAT IIs until an appropriate achievement-oriented test could be developed to replace the SAT I. The text of that speech was a closely held secret; I shared it with only a few trusted colleagues.

I flew to Washington, D.C., on a Friday, with the speech scheduled for Sunday afternoon. I checked into my hotel Friday evening. The next morning I woke up, planning to spend an enjoyable Saturday visiting the Hirshhorn Gallery. When I opened my hotel door, there in the hallway was the *Washington Post*. The headline on the front-page story—top of the fold—read: "Key

SAT Test Under Fire in Calif.; University President Proposes New Admissions Criteria." I rushed out to retrieve copies of the *Los Angeles Times* and the *Chicago Tribune* and found the same thing: front-page stories. The *New York Times* had a long story, also starting on the front page, with a headline that read, "Head of U. of California Seeks to End SAT Use in Admissions." The story was particularly interesting because they had reproduced word-for-word almost half of the speech.

I will take a moment to explain how this happened. A young man in the U.C. press office was about to take another job, and he had friends at the Associated Press. The computer system in my office was not as secure as we had assumed, and he was able to obtain the next-to-last draft of the speech. I know this because, at the last moment, Pat Hayashi convinced me to add a paragraph on comprehensive review, namely, that the University of California should stress the importance of multiple factors in the admissions process and not rely too heavily on test scores. So I said, "OK, draft a paragraph and put it in." And he did. When I saw the paragraph, I was satisfied, except that he used the term *holistic review.* I dislike the word *holistic,* with its various connotations, and quickly changed it to "comprehensive review." But the *New York Times* carried the term *holistic* because they had the penultimate draft of the speech. That term continues to plague me even to this day. Apparently, some people still refer to the original *New York Times* account.

I never made it to the Hirshhorn on Saturday. Most of the day was spent trying to dodge reporters and frantic calls from U.C. officials. When I arrived at the ACE meetings on Sunday afternoon, the auditorium was packed, as were the overflow rooms. The place was alive with reporters. There were TV cameras and satellite feeds everywhere; it was truly a chaotic scene. Stan Ikenberry, the president of ACE, was absolutely delighted. This was the biggest crowd and the most media coverage ACE had ever had. No one seemed disturbed that the speech had been leaked to the press the day before.

The audience's response was wonderful! I had expected to attract some attention in the higher-education community, but I was unprepared for the general public's response. Clearly the topic hit a deep chord in the American psyche.

Over the course of the next several months, I received hundreds of letters from people describing their experiences with the SAT. I was on *The NewsHour with Jim Lehrer;* I was in a debate on *Good Morning America.* The major magazines, such as *Newsweek* and *U.S. News & World Report,* had cover stories. The one I liked best was *Time* magazine; they devoted a large part of an issue to the subject of college admissions testing. Nicholas Lemann, a reporter who authored the book *The Big Test: The Secret History of the American Meritocracy,* wrote one of the *Time* magazine articles that I particularly like. The piece includes a photograph of me on one page, and facing me on the opposite page is the president of the United States, George W. Bush. The question over the photos is, "What Do These Two Men Have in Common?" Lemann's answer was that we both supported the idea of standardized testing. A few clever souls speculated that what the two of us had in common was the same SAT score. Fortunately, I was able to respond, "No, that's not the case. I was a student at the University of Chicago, which, at that time, had its own entrance exam, and it certainly wasn't the SAT."

Some people assumed that I was arguing for no testing at all; they hadn't bothered to read the actual speech. For a few weeks, anti-testing groups saw me as a hero, until they realized that I was not proposing a ban on standardized testing.

Unfortunately, in one discussion with reporters, I described the impact of my granddaughter's experience on my thinking, and after that she was often mentioned in their stories. She was embarrassed by the attention and not too happy with her grandfather. I'll return to her views on this matter later.

The College Board's response to my speech was less than enthusiastic. There were some sharp exchanges in the press, and a number of SAT supporters wrote scathing articles; a few got a little too personal. Some of the articles were written by college admissions officers who failed to disclose that they had been paid consultants to the College Board. And efforts were made to enlist key U.C. faculty to oppose the proposal. But, as I will explain later, the College Board did, in the end, agree to totally overhaul the SAT. The president of the College Board, Gaston Caperton, deserves much of the credit for what took place. He had served as the governor of West Virginia and in that role had been particularly effective in improving K-12 education. As the SAT debate evolved, he showed remarkable leadership. Some of the senior people at the College Board wanted to maintain the status quo, but as Caperton immersed himself in the issue, his perspectives changed and he concluded that a major overhaul of the test was needed. I admire Caperton greatly. He showed courage and leadership, and the forthcoming changes in the SAT I would not have occurred without his involvement.

Buried in the ACE speech was a very brief paragraph—five sentences that were overlooked by most people. It noted that the University of California had used the SAT I and three SAT IIs for a number of years, and that several small-scale U.C.

studies indicated that the SAT II was the better predictor of college performance. Just a brief paragraph, hardly noticed, but it was a ticking time bomb.

At this point it will be useful to provide some history. The U.C. faculty, under the University's tradition of shared governance, have responsibility for the admissions process. That responsibility is exercised by the Board of Admissions and Relations with Schools (BOARS) of the U.C. Academic Senate. In 1960, when many universities had already adopted the SAT, U.C. still did not require the test in its admissions process. BOARS, at that time, launched a study to compare the SAT and several achievement tests as predictors of college performance. The results were mixed. The achievement tests proved a more useful predictor of success than did the SAT, but the benefit of both tests appeared marginal. BOARS decided not to introduce admissions tests and to continue to rely on high school grades.

In 1968, U.C. began requiring the SAT I and three SAT II achievement tests, although the applicant's SAT scores were not considered in the regular admissions process. However, in special cases, high SAT scores were a way of admitting promising students whose high school grades fell below the U.C. standard. U.C. requires applicants to take a specific set of courses in high school; poor grades in these courses could be offset by high SAT scores. Lemann, in his book *The Big Test,* asserts that U.C.'s adoption of the SAT was a turning point for the College Board. Once U.C. required the test, the SAT became the gold standard for admissions tests. To this day, more students applying to U.C. take the SAT than at any other institution.

By 1979, U.C. faced increasing enrollment pressures and finally adopted the SAT as a formal part of the regular admissions process. That year, BOARS established U.C.'s Eligibility Index: a sliding scale combining the high school grade-point average with the SAT I score to determine whether a student is U.C. eligible. The Eligibility Index was established because several studies showed U.C. accepted students well below its mandated top 12.5 percent of statewide high school graduates. Note that only the SAT I score was included in the Eligibility Index, even though applicants were still required to take three SAT II tests. All eligible students were guaranteed acceptance at one of the U.C. campuses, but not necessarily the campus of their choice. Campus admissions officers at each of the U.C. campuses used the full array of data, including the SAT II scores, in making individual campus decisions.

In 1995, shortly after I became president, BOARS—with my strong endorsement—redefined the Eligibility Index to include GPA plus scores on the SAT I and three SAT IIs (writing, mathematics, and a third test of the student's choice). This was done on the basis of several small-scale studies suggesting that the SAT IIs were good predictors of college success. BOARS established a weighting scheme that had the principal weight on the GPA, but with a relative weight of 1 on the SAT I compared with a weight of 3 on the SAT IIs. So, in 1995, the word went out to high school students and their counselors that the SAT II had taken on a new significance.

By the time I gave my ACE speech, we had four years of data under the new policy on all freshmen who were admitted to and subsequently enrolled at a U.C. campus. We had approximately seventy-eight thousand student protocols. A protocol included the student's high school grades, SAT I scores (verbal and quantitative), three SAT II scores, family income, family educational background, the quality of the high school the student attended, race or ethnicity, and several other variables. And, of course, the protocol included the grade record of the student in her or his freshman year at a U.C. campus.

When I gave my ACE speech, an analysis of the U.C. data was not yet available. However, a few months later, two researchers at the U.C. Office of the President, Saul Geiser and Roger Studley, completed a seminal study on predictive validity using the data set. The study examined the effectiveness of high school grades and various combinations of SAT I and SAT II scores in predicting success in college. A full account of the study has been published in the journal *Educational Assessment* and is available on the U.C. Web site.[2]

In brief, the study shows that the SAT II is a far better predictor of college grades than the SAT I. The combination of high school grades and the three SAT IIs accounts for 22.2 percent of the variance in first-year college grades. When the SAT I is added to the combination of high school grades and the SAT IIs, the explained variance increases from 22.2 percent to 22.3 percent, a trivial increment.

The data indicate that the predictive validity of the SAT II is much less affected by differences in socioeconomic background than is the SAT I. After controlling for family income and parents' education, the predictive power of the SAT II is undiminished, whereas the relationship between SAT I scores and U.C. grades virtually disappears. The SAT II is not only a better predictor, but also a fairer test insofar as it is demonstrably less sensitive than the SAT I to differences in family income and parents' education.

These findings for the full U.C. data set hold equally well for three major disciplinary subsets of the data, namely for (1) physical sciences, mathematics, and engineering, (2) biological sciences, and (3) social sciences and humanities. Across these disciplinary areas, the SAT II is consistently a better predictor of student performance than the SAT I.

Analyses with respect to the racial-ethnic impact of the SAT I versus the SAT II indicate that, in general, there are only minor differences between the tests. The SAT II is a better predictor of U.C. grades for most racial-ethnic groups than the SAT I, but both tests tend to overpredict freshman grades for underrepresented minorities to a small but measurable extent. Eliminating the SAT I in favor of the SAT II would have little effect on rates of U.C. eligibility and admissions for students from different racial-ethnic groups.

The U.C. data yield another interesting result. Of the various tests that make up the SAT I (verbal and quantitative) and the three SAT IIs, the best single predictor of student performance was the SAT II writing test. Given the importance of writing ability at the college level, it should not be surprising that a test of actual writing skills correlates strongly with college grades.

Once the Geiser-Studley study was made public, opposition to a change in the SAT I quickly died out. And the U.C. faculty were fully engaged in planning for a new admissions test. In March 2002, Gaston Caperton, in his role as president of the College Board, announced that they would eliminate the SAT I as it then stood and replace it—on a nationwide basis—with a new test very much in accord with my original proposal and the planning that the U.C. faculty had already done.

Since then, the College Board has been consulting with U.C. faculty and other groups around the country about the new test. The test that is now being developed includes a twenty-five-minute essay requiring students to produce an actual writing sample, a more substantial mathematics section assessing higher-level mathematical skills, and a reading comprehension section that does not include verbal analogies. I believe this is an excellent solution that reflects the changes called for in my ACE speech.

When I look back, I'm amazed at the speed with which change has occurred. The ACE speech was in February 2001, the College Board made its decision to overhaul the SAT I in March of 2002, and the new test is now being field-tested and will be in use for students entering college in fall 2006. In a brief time, college admissions will have undergone a revolutionary change—a change that will affect millions of young people.

My granddaughter will be in the first group of high school students to take the new SAT I. As a sophomore she took the PSAT—a test preparatory to taking the old SAT I—and did brilliantly. She was not hesitant to accuse me of complicating her future. Her high school quickly adjusted to the proposed changes and now has students writing a twenty-five-minute essay once a week in preparation for the new test.

One of the clear lessons of history is that colleges and universities, through their admissions requirements, strongly influence what is taught in the schools. From my viewpoint, the most important reason for changing the SAT is to send a clear message to K-12 students, their teachers, and parents that learning to write and mastering a solid background in mathematics are of critical importance. The changes that are being made in the SAT go a long way toward accomplishing that goal.

NOTES

These remarks were delivered as the invited address to the annual meeting of the American Educational Research Association in San Diego, April 14, 2004, and subsequently published by the American Psychological Society in *Observer* 18, no. 5 (May 2005): 15–22. Reprinted with permission.

1. http://www.ucop.edu/news/sat/speech1.html.

2. http://www.ucop.edu/sas/research/researchandplanning/pdf/sat_study.pdf.

Farewell Remarks to the Board of Regents

September 2003

Very shortly, I will be leaving the presidency of the University of California after eight years in office. It has been pointed out that I seem to have a knack for picking tumultuous times for my entrances and exits. When I took office as U.C.'s seventeenth president in 1995, the University and much of the state were paralyzed by a bitter debate over affirmative action. As I prepare to leave on October 1, our state is consumed by a gubernatorial recall election that will feature a ballot with 135 candidates. California never is at a loss for interesting issues.

As I reflect on my time as president and look to the future of the University, two major themes become apparent. First, the things that have been achieved at the University of California are nothing short of stunning. The U.C. system today is one of the world's leading centers of higher learning, and its accomplishments as a public university in the United States are unsurpassed. These accomplishments are not attributable to any individual president—they are far too great for any one person to claim responsibility—but rather are the product of a talented and committed community of faculty, staff, students, parents, alumni, Regents, friends, and supporters. The skill and energy of this community of people are reason alone for optimism about the University of California's future.

Second, however, it would be a mistake to discount the challenges that lie ahead. In particular, the State of California's fiscal distress, and the threat of a downward spiral in state financial support for the University, will make the next few years a period of great consequence for the University of California. What we are, and how valuable we are to the people of the state, will be thoroughly tested.

This is a great university, astonishing in many respects. It also is, today, a university facing great risk. We are confronting a number of individual challenges, each of which could be survived in isolation, but when taken together, they threaten to undermine U.C.'s foundation of quality, accessibility, and affordability.

Several years ago, in a piece entitled "The Future of the University of California" [included in this volume], I wrote the following: "The role of knowledge in transforming virtually every aspect of our world has moved research universities like the University of California to center stage of American life. More than any other institution in our society, research universities are on the cutting edge in producing the well-educated people who drive our economy and the new research ideas that keep it growing."

The University of California is a leading example of the phenomenon I was describing. Our faculty are, by numerous measures, national and international leaders in the quality and productivity of their research. For California students, U.C. offers an opportunity to gain a world-class research-based education right here in California, taught by world leaders in every field of academic inquiry. We are a community devoted to learning—not for learning's sake alone, but for the sake of enhancing scientific progress, cultural understanding, and quality of life in the society around us. This institution, no ivory tower, leaves a deep mark on the state that supports it.

Economically, we contribute highly trained graduates and research innovations that fuel the creation of companies, jobs, and entire new industries. More broadly, our agricultural programs, medical centers, extension programs, and K-12 outreach initiatives bring the University into homes and schools and fields throughout the state of California.

Together, over the last several years, we have built on this foundation of excellence. With the implementation of Eligibility in the Local Context and Comprehensive Review, we have updated our admissions policies to ensure that they draw in high-achieving students from all corners of the state and all educational backgrounds. Our efforts with the California Community Colleges to increase transfers to U.C. are proving similarly successful, and the Dual Admissions Program will offer an additional route to transfer success. Our work with the College Board and ACT has led to improved national admissions tests and a closer relationship between what students are taught in high school and what they are tested on for college entrance. The University's impact on the California economy has been magnified through the California Institutes for Science and Innovation, the Industry-University Cooperative Research Program, and our expansion of engineering and computer science enrollments by more than 70 percent.

We have continued to attract faculty of the highest quality, along with exceptionally qualified students, and we have enhanced our educational offerings by expanding freshman seminars and introducing a new degree, the Master of Advanced Study, for working adults. We launched a new initiative to increase enrollments of graduate students after years of stasis. Federal research funding has set new records, and private donations to the University topped the one-billion-dollar mark in a single year for the first time ever.

Our California Digital Library represents a groundbreaking effort to pool the resources of the U.C. libraries, make their collections available electronically to the broadest possible audience, and give faculty members new options for disseminating their work. We have sought to improve working conditions for our faculty and staff by providing health benefits for domestic partners, new initiatives to promote gender equity, expansion of child care facilities, and programs to help offset lagging salary funding from the state. And all of this has occurred amid explosive student enrollment growth and the founding of a tenth campus, U.C. Merced—the University's first new campus in forty years.

My concerns for the future are largely tied to the State of California's finances and the vulnerability of public higher education to further budget cuts. The cuts that have occurred already are very real, and they will have deep impacts—in areas ranging from teaching to research to outreach to Cooperative Extension. Over the last three years, the University's net state-funded budget has fallen nearly 14 percent, while enrollments have steadily increased. Student fees are rising sharply, employee positions are being lost, and faculty and staff salaries are falling behind where they should be in order to maintain quality programs. More ominous, however, is the possibility of even deeper cuts in the coming years. Given the depth of the cuts that have occurred already, the options left for absorbing deeper cuts are perilous: reduce access for qualified students, reduce the quality of the academic program, or raise student fees even further. None of these options is attractive; all will be roundly criticized; and one or more of them will have to be pursued if the recent trend of state disinvestment in the University continues.

Of particular concern is the fact that these cuts come at a time of substantial enrollment growth, as California's college-age population continues to swell. Already, there are indications that the state may be forced to stop funding enrollment growth or cost increases of any kind. This is a distressing turn of events because, for the last forty-three years under the Master Plan for Higher Education, the State of California and the University of California have guaranteed a place for every student who meets our eligibility requirements. The reduction of state funding will seriously challenge our joint ability to meet that historic promise.

Economic expansion and contraction are cyclical. My own presidency began with the economic crisis of the early to mid-1990s, and it is ending with a new economic crisis in the first decade of the new century. When things are bad, we can be assured they at least will not last forever; California will regain its financial footing. The question is what will be lost in the meantime, particularly at institutions such as the University of California that are relatively unprotected in the state budget process. Quality, access, and affordability—the defining characteristics of the University of California—are at risk today, and once lost, they will not be easy to regain. I hope the state's leaders will confront this issue thoughtfully as they deliberate on future budgets.

A second concern for the future is diversity. As noted earlier, I came into office just after the Regents approved Resolution SP-1 and as voters were preparing to approve Proposition 209, forbidding the consideration of race and ethnicity in University admissions, among other things. I continue to believe those were the wrong decisions. As I wrote in the *Washington Post* not long ago [the op-ed "Diversity: Not There Yet" is included in this volume], "We have pursued both excellence and diversity because we believe they are inextricably linked, and because we know that an institution that ignores either of them runs the risk of becoming irrelevant in a state with the knowledge-based economy and tremendously varied population of California." Without the ability to take race into account in the admissions process, we have turned to other approaches for ensuring educational opportunity for high-achieving students of all backgrounds. The Eligibility in the Local Context program has been successful, particularly in expanding access for students who excel in educationally disadvantaged environments. Our programs working with public schools and teachers to improve academic performance and college eligibility have shown promising results as well, but instead of receiving the long-term support they need, these programs have been subjected to dramatic changes in funding.

State funding for U.C. outreach and teacher professional development stood at 32 million dollars in 1997–98, soared to 184 million dollars in 2000–01, and since has plummeted to 43 million dollars in 2003–04.

The good news is that student diversity has, indeed, increased following the dramatic drop after the initial implementation of SP-1. But the proportions of Latino and African American students at our most selective campuses remain far below their previous levels, and the gap between the diversity of the overall U.C. freshman class and the diversity of California's high school graduates is widening. Politically, the University is caught between those who advocate increasing diversity at any cost and those who seek any opportunity to prove we are flouting Proposition 209. And I worry that students and parents, in this superheated environment, may focus too much on whether there is some "trick" to being admitted to our campuses, rather than concentrating on the academic performance and personal achievement that matter most.

We have made great progress over the last eight years, more than I would have predicted when I took office. But as our state continues to diversify—Latinos will increase as a proportion of California's public school population from 34 percent in 1990 to 52 percent in 2010—we must continue working to ensure that we are accessible to the hardest-working and highest-achieving students from all backgrounds in our state. There are no simple ways to achieve this result, particularly if budget-driven enrollment constraints force a reduction in access overall. But our success or lack thereof will have a direct impact on the University's public, political, and budgetary support. More importantly, it will have a direct impact on the lives of the next generation of

Californians—the students we are counting on to ensure our state's future.

A final point about the challenges ahead concerns the national laboratories we manage for the federal government. The Lawrence Berkeley, Lawrence Livermore, and Los Alamos national laboratories have played a decisive role in the modern history of our nation, and I am extremely proud of their association with the University. Their achievements across a broad spectrum of scientific inquiry—national security, the environment, astronomy, human health, and countless other areas—are thoroughly impressive. For its part, the University has never gained financially from the relationship but has managed the laboratories as a national service. During the last year, we have been working through a series of management problems, particularly at Los Alamos. The result has been a needed intensification of the University's presence and guidance at the laboratories, along with a range of improvements to the business and administrative practices of the laboratory system. These changes are a significant accomplishment, and I am in the debt of all who worked to make them happen.

In the coming months, the University will be faced with the choice of whether to compete for one or more of these contracts with the Department of Energy. I want to see the relationship continue. But we must assess objectively the terms of the competition to ascertain if they are fair and meet the requirements for an effective relationship. I have no doubt that if the University chooses to compete for these contracts, it will do so successfully. Whether that outcome will be in the University's interest—whether the terms of the competition will make continued management of the labs consistent with our mission—is yet to be determined.

I am deeply honored to have had the opportunity to serve the University of California, and I remain optimistic about its future. I believe in California, its people, and their capacity to make the right choices. And in today's knowledge-based society, the University of California is key to the prosperity and well-being of our people. But the future holds many challenges, and the University must plan effectively to meet these challenges. My successor, Bob Dynes, is superbly qualified to lead this effort. He will need the support and assistance of all who are a part of the University of California.

One hundred thirty-five years ago, some farsighted and public-minded Californians created a university for the people of their state. The establishment of a new university was not an uncommon development in the nineteenth-century United States, but in California it had an uncommon result. Here, on the western frontier, in a land of boundless optimism and limitless energy, the University of California grew from the simplest of origins to become one of the world's great universities—an institution that powers economic growth, enriches lives, advances knowledge, and invigorates the spirit. It is perhaps the only public university in the nation that has stayed competitive with the most prestigious private universities, and it has done so while maintaining its commitment to providing an education to every young person, from every walk of life, who works hard to become eligible.

The University of California could have become a widely accessible and good, but not great, university. Or, it could have become a great, but highly exclusive, university. The genius of the California experience is that we have created a university that is both great and accessible—a public university that fulfills a distinctly American vision of democracy and meritocracy. What happens to this University next is up to all of us—the U.C. community, the political leadership, and the people of California—for we are, all of us, its trustees.

Regents' Resolution in Honor of Richard C. Atkinson

September 2003

WHEREAS, on October 2, 2003, Richard C. Atkinson will have retired as the seventeenth President of the University of California, the fifth-longest serving president in the University's rich history, and a president whose dynamic and courageous leadership has enhanced U.C.'s stature as the world's leading research university of the twenty-first century; and

WHEREAS, in the tradition of Benjamin Franklin and Vannevar Bush, he has contributed brilliantly to the nation and this state as an inventor, public servant, and visionary leader, advancing the frontiers of science through his pathbreaking explorations of human cognition, through his successful efforts to build new bridges between universities and industry, through his vigorous advocacy of academic measures that are equal to the complexity of human talent, and in defining and defending the role of the scientific enterprise in the American Century and beyond; and

WHEREAS, his distinguished contributions as a member of the academy were instrumental in his appointment by President Jimmy Carter as the director of the National Science Foundation, a position he used to breathe new life into the foundation at a time when it had lost the confidence of Congress, initiating the first U.S.-China student and scholar exchange program, establishing engineering as an area for funding on a par with the sciences, and revitalizing the foundation's efforts with respect to science education, thus renewing the foundation as a national treasure for generations of scientists to come; and

WHEREAS, the Regents of the University of California recognized an unparalleled combination of outstanding administrative skills, clear vision, and scientific brilliance when, in 1980, he was selected as the fifth chancellor of U.C. San Diego, where he set an unparalleled standard of excellence, leading the campus with vigor and determination, recruiting and building a sterling faculty, greatly increasing student enrollment, providing faculty and students with world-class facilities, and building innovative university-industry relationships, all of which served to transform the campus from a well-respected center of learning into a world-class institution of higher education; and

WHEREAS, in 1995, he became the seventeenth president of the University of California, and as such has been a dynamic and imaginative leader, boldly guiding the University to new heights of greatness through his unceasing devotion to expanding access to the University for an increasingly diverse population, forging historic new admissions policies in order to make the University, as he has said, demonstrably inclusive and fair, enhancing the excellence of its faculty, advancing pioneering research initiatives that were begun under his thoughtful guidance, building enrollment in fields vital to the future of the state, and making the dream of U.C. Merced a reality; and

WHEREAS, a dominant force nationally and internationally in higher education, his uncommon skill in identifying and solving complex and difficult problems has led to his successful efforts in revolutionizing standardized testing in the United States and beyond, providing a myriad of opportunities for all those who seek to better themselves through education, and improving and enhancing classroom and administrative skills for K-12 teachers and administrators, thus making the State of California a place where in the future each child will be afforded a greater opportunity of a sound education;

NOW, THEREFORE BE IT RESOLVED, that the Regents of the University of California express to Richard C. Atkinson their lasting gratitude and heartfelt appreciation for his extraordinary stewardship of the University, his steadfast adherence to excellence, and his unfailing commitment to the highest ideals of the academic enterprise, and to his wife, Rita, for her thoughtful contributions to the life of the University, as well as for the indispensable role she has played as presidential partner and counselor;

AND BE IT FURTHER RESOLVED that the Regents extend to Rita and Dick Atkinson their best wishes as they leave the presidency for a life rich in the company of family and good friends and further direct that a suitably inscribed copy of this resolution be presented to them as a token of the Board's high regard and genuine affection for these valued friends, who will be greatly missed and affectionately remembered.

INDEX

Text:	11/15 Granjon
Display:	Granjon
Compositor:	IBT Global
Indexer:	Kevin Millham
Illustrator:	Bill Nelson
Printer and binder:	IBT Global